GARDENERS' WORLD

VEGETABLES FOR SMALL GARDENS

GARDENERS' WORLD

VEGETABLES FOR SMALL GARDENS

LYNDA BROWN

BBC BOOKS

For Alan and Jackie

ACKNOWLEDGEMENTS

Gardeners are generous by nature; to experience this first hand in the course of writing his book has been a great privilege and pleasure. My sincere thanks to all who have shared their knowledge and skill with me. I should also like to thank Ian Spence and Carol Woods at Barnsdale, whose expertise and hard work made the Cook's Garden possible. Finally, to my editor Nicky Copeland, for her unfailing sunny outlook and her painstaking diligence, many fond thanks.

PICTURE CREDITS

Garden Picture Library pages 7 (Brigitte Thomas) and 45 (Brian Carter); **John Glover** page 77; **Stephen Hamilton** pages 3, 21, 35 and 109; **Andrew Lawson** page 95; **Clay Perry** page 38; **Photos Horticultural** pages 11, 13 and 27.

Colour illustrations by Gordon Munro

Published by BBC Books,
a division of BBC Enterprises Limited,
Woodlands, 80 Wood Lane,
London W12 0TT

First Published 1993

© Lynda Brown 1993

ISBN 0 563 36466 1

Designed by Roger Daniels
Black and white illustrations by Sue Rose
Set in 10/13 Kennerley by Ace Filmsetting Ltd
Printed and bound in Great Britain by
Clays Ltd, St Ives Plc
Colour separation by Dot Gradations Ltd
Cover printed by Clays Ltd, St Ives Plc

CONTENTS

INTRODUCTION

This book is about growing vegetables, salads and herbs in small gardens, both for inexperienced gardeners and for gardeners who have never grown vegetables before because they thought there was not enough room in the garden. Its aims are very simple: to show how cultivating a kitchen garden can fit easily into busy lives; and to encourage and help you to get the best out of your garden no matter how small it is or how little time you may have.

It's not necessary to be self-sufficient or devote all of every weekend to producing enough vegetables to feed the family. The beauty of growing vegetables in small gardens is that you can have the best of both worlds. By choosing crops which are easy to grow, focusing on varieties for flavour, and including vegetables that are expensive to buy or unusual crops that are not readily available, you can create a modern kitchen garden providing a wide variety of fresh home-grown vegetables with true gourmet taste. These supplement shop-bought vegetables and, together with the pleasure they bring, the garden more than pays for itself. Because it is small, moreover, it takes little time, is manageable and fun to do.

The book is divided into two parts, designed to be used in conjunction with each other. The first part covers basic gardening know-how and techniques; the second, individual crops, including a chapter on those suitable for growing in containers. Each entry includes cultivation details, advice on harvesting and culinary tips. It also includes an approximate idea of how many plants to grow to give you a reasonable crop to use as a yardstick.

I have chosen a wide variety of vegetables, salad plants and herbs that are well-suited to small gardens and are easy and straightforward to grow. I have not included very large vegetables, such as sweetcorn; or vegetables which are known to be difficult,

A delightful, small, sheltered bed in a cottage garden showing a variety of summer vegetables, herbs and salad plants, including spinach, sugar snap peas and lettuce. In the background are large terracotta pots for forcing seakale or rhubarb.

such as cauliflower; or, regrettably, one or two vegetables such as broad beans which are delicious but which, on balance, give too small a yield for the space they occupy.

MAKING IT WORK

The main diference between growing vegetables in a small garden and having a large vegetable plot is not scale but attitude. In a traditional garden, the emphasis has always been to grow as much as you can as big as you can. For modern small gardens this isn't applicable, or desirable. Instead, you tailor your growing to suit. Within the confines of the space available, you only grow what you want and what you need, and concentrate on variety, enjoyment and flavour.

With a little planning, a small garden can easily accommodate a selection from each of the major groups of vegetables, as well as tomatoes, peppers and so on, without any difficulty at all. I have given suggestions, but the final choice is yours. You won't be able to grow everything, or grow vast quantities, but you will certainly be able to grow sufficient to make it worthwhile. As a general guideline, choose a few from each of the main categories, increasing your range gradually as you gain experience and learn to assess which crops are best for you. You may want to concentrate on unusual salad crops, for example, or find that what you most appreciate is having fresh garden vegetables in winter. The thing is not to be hidebound

by convention; in small gardens, as long as you make choices, anything is possible.

By far the best way to grow vegetables in small gardens is to use the raised bed system (see p. 20). It looks good and allows you to grow vegetables intensively, and the beds are easy to maintain. I have been growing vegetables for 12 years now using this method and would never grow them any other way. Looking after your soil and plants properly is the other key to success – for this always comes through in the flavour and ultimate eating-quality of vegetables. Build up the fertility of your soil, get to know the basic needs of plants and how each individual task fits into the overall scheme, and you will be well on the way to success.

This brings me neatly to organic gardening, which I also believe is ideal for small gardens and the best way to achieve lasting success. Gardening organically simply means gardening in harmony with nature, working with, rather than against, the ecological balance of the garden and environment. In the organic system, the soil is the most important asset a gardener has. A healthy soil means healthy crops full of flavour; and healthy crops mean healthy people.

I do find gardening organically is easier in small gardens, where everything is manageable and interacts closely. I believe it's also the surest way to get the best results when you are growing intensively, when soil condition and fertility are of paramount importance. In practice, however, especially in small gardens where every lettuce really matters, it's a question of doing the very best you can given your own circumstances. So although I have given organic solutions wherever possible, don't feel guilty if you buy the occasional bottle of inorganic fertilizer, or feel you have to resort to slug pellets, especially if you are new to gardening. Otherwise, you may risk being put off the very real advantages of organic gardening before it has had time to prove itself. The best way to learn about it is to join the Henry Doubleday Research Association at Ryton Organic Gardens. I have been a member for 17 years and recommend it highly; you will find the address on p. 123.

Finally, as every gardener knows, despite their best endeavours, the weather is the joker in the pack; but don't worry, the sun always shines next year. Happy gardening and happy cooking!

1

GETTING STARTED

Creating a small kitchen garden plot is an exciting venture. It doesn't require much in the way of specialized equipment, or a heavy financial outlay, but for really successful results, there are several basic considerations and gardening techniques which all play their part and are just as important as deciding which vegetables to grow and how to grow them.

SITE AND LOCATION

Vegetables do not grow well in shady, cold or damp places. Although it seems an obvious point to make, a sunny, sheltered plot is by far the best location; of the two, shelter is almost more important than sun, for vegetables sheltered from even light winds can increase their yields up to as much as 50 per cent. If your position is very exposed, you should consider some form of windbreak.

Fortunately, small gardens often have the advantage over large gardens in this respect; they tend to be contained, often surrounded by fencing or closed in by other houses, and therefore afford a reasonable degre of shelter. But it's still surprising how much climatic variation there can be within even a small garden. To a certain extent, each garden has its own micro-climate and it is important to be aware of this, earmarking spots which may be suitable for particular plants – a sunny spot to stand tomatoes, or a damp place to put the mint, and so on.

When planning your garden, choose the best possible location you can for your vegetable plot, one with the maximum light and the most shelter. Light is more important than heat (a baking hot spot will cause almost as many problems as a cold, damp one). Don't be put off, however, if the plot is shaded for part of the day. Although few vegetables grow satisfactorily in shade, you don't need bright sunlight all day.

Newly established deep beds with paths between them in a sunny position in a small garden. Summer lettuces are being grown as a catch crop on top of the celery trench and, in the foreground, courgettes are ready for harvesting. A small patch of strawberries is sheltered by the greenhouse, protected by black netting.

REGIONAL VARIATION

Which part of the country you live in can make a marked difference to how you plan your gardening calendar and even which crops you grow. The best advice is to get to know your garden, for it will tell you better than any gardening book what are the right sowing and planting times for you. Never think that cropping plans, which seem like a great idea, especially to a beginner, are sacrosanct and rigid; learn to work with the seasons that present themselves and adapt your gardening requirements accordingly. This way you can gradually narrow down which crops and which varieties of each crop are most successful, and your cropping plan can be tailor-made to suit yourself.

CITY GARDENS

Gardens in cities have their own advantages and disadvantages. They are often sheltered, snugly surrounded by high walls (ideal for growing beans) or by other houses, which usually means they are less exposed and may have a warmer micro-environment. It also means they may be shaded and the soil may be poor; more than a few city gardeners have dug down to find their gardens full of old bedsteads, broken china and rubble instead of earth. Access may be difficult; humping bags of organic matter, and assorted gardening paraphernalia, through the front of the house in order to reach the garden is no fun.

We have done it and I do not particularly recommend it. How convenient it is to water crops should also be taken into account. But perhaps the factor that worries new gardeners most is pollution. What effect does this have on the crops? Is it worth growing crops in cities?

Unless very severe, each of these problems can be overcome to a greater or lesser extent, and for every city garden that is not suitable for growing vegetables for one reason or another, there is a shining example which provides inspiration for us all. You need to assess the strengths and weaknesses of your garden and, having taken the decision to go ahead, you can then set about the work of putting any problems right.

SHADE

If the garden is heavily shaded and there is no way of improving the light – by removing a tree or any large shrubs, for example – it is better to restrict yourself to a few herbs and container-grown plants (see p. 108) which you can put in whatever sunny position you have at your disposal, such as a balcony, patio or doorstep.

Otherwise, position the vegetable plot in the part of the garden that receives most

A productive city garden shielded by a wall showing healthy kohl rabi, cabbages, French beans and peas supported by traditional twig pea sticks. The path is edged with chervil, a favourite edging plant for vegetable beds since the seventeenth century.

light; a spot with full light in the morning and shade in the afternoon is far preferable to a north-facing area which is slow to warm up and only receives sun in the afternoon. Trees and shrubs take a lot of nutrients and, even more important, moisture from the soil. As far as possible, crops should be grown well apart from both.

Some vegetables are more tolerant of shade. These include radish, kohl rabi, endive, chicory, claytonia, land cress, sorrel, spinach and spinach beet.

ACCESS

In almost all cases, this is the one thing you will have to grin and bear. Before you buy garden equipment, make sure large items such as the wheelbarrow and compost bin go through the front (and back) door. Choose a greenhouse or garden shed that comes as a flat-pack, and check that the supplier is prepared to erect it on site if necessary.

WATERING

An outside tap is a godsend. If this is not possible, a long garden hose (buy it longer than you need to allow for awkward corners you forgot about) is invaluable. Watering routines are discussed on pp. 39–40.

POLLUTION

Pollution is a fact of life, a problem for all gardeners, not just those growing crops in built-up areas. For city gardens, the main concern has centred on the plants' uptake of lead, often present in significant quantities due to traffic emissions. This applies to any crops grown near roads, wherever you live, especially those within 22–55 yards (20–50 metres) of busy traffic. If you are at all concerned, lead levels can be measured by the local Environmental Health Department. The Wessex Environmental Consultancy (address on p. 123) also specializes in lead soil analysis.

Lead is a major pollutant. It persists in the soil indefinitely, is toxic, and can cause impaired mental development in babies and children. Lead is also toxic to plants, but most have effective barrier mechanisms which prevent uptake through the roots, so unless soil levels are very high, uptake of lead is not likely to be a significant risk. As a general guideline, soils with lead levels of 300–500 mg/Kg should not be used for growing crops; special care should be taken where lead levels show 100 mg/Kg and above.

Surface contamination of lead in the atmosphere settling on the leaves and skins of the vegetables can be a problem. Crops at particular risk are leafy crops such as lettuce, cabbage and spinach. Outer leaves are polluted more than inner leaves. The skins of root crops grown in contaminated soils can also be infected.

The following points are useful safeguards to help you prevent contamination of your crops:

● Don't grow crops near a busy road; if this is unavoidable, a tall evergreen hedge will help to block lead particles and reduce the level of contamination.

● Dig lots of organic matter into the soil: this binds the lead, making it less available to the plants. Acid soils favour uptake of lead; ensure the pH is 6.5–7, adding lime if necessary.

● Grow leafy crops under a protective cover such as horticultural fleece (see pp. 37–8) or cloches.

● Wash *all* vegetables *very* thoroughly to remove surface dust and all traces of soil. Root crops should be peeled and the outer leaves of crops such as lettuce and cabbage should be discarded if you are concerned about possible contamination.

SOIL

Soil is the second critical starting point in any garden. No matter what kind of soil the garden has, it can *always* be improved by adding sufficient organic matter.

The ideal soil is a rich, dark crumbly loam that is high in organic matter, moist but free-draining, and fertile. Such a soil provides the best conditions for soil life, root growth, and hence healthy plants. Most of us, however, start with considerably less than ideal soils. It's important to recognize your soil type,

and soil structure, because it has a direct bearing on how crops will perform. The two main types are sandy soils and clay soils – most soils are somewhere in between, usually predominantly one type or another. Often the soil in one part of the garden will be different in composition, and may be poorer or better than the rest. Again, you should take note of this.

SANDY SOIL

Sandy soil tends to be light in colour, free-draining and feels gritty to the touch. It is easy to work and warms up more quickly than other soils, but is less fertile. It needs plenty of organic matter to improve humus content and water retention, and regular applications of organic fertilizer or compost to increase fertility. Mulching the plants with a layer of organic matter to prevent evaporation of water can also help. Early crops and root vegetables do well in sandy soils. Courgettes are likely to do less well.

CLAY SOIL

A clay soil is the polar opposite of a sandy soil. It is darker, does not drain as easily and often feels sticky to the touch. It is heavy and difficult to work, forming clods that do not break down easily, cold when wet, sets hard when dry, but is inherently a fertile soil. In spring it takes longer (approximately two to three weeks) to warm up than a sandy soil, so sowing and planting times should be delayed to allow for this. It also needs plenty of organic matter to make it more friable, and to improve drainage. Avoid digging when it is very wet or very dry, which will harm the soil further (and is harder work), and avoid walking on the soil whenever possible, as this compacts it. Use cloches, polythene or horticultural fleece (see pp. 37–8) to warm the soil before sowing or planting, and use fine compost on the surface of the soil to sow and cover the seeds.

Brassicas generally do very well on clay soils, with kale being most tolerant of poor conditions. Vigorous summer crops that can be transplanted rather than being sown direct, such as Swiss chard and courgettes, cope with clay, but early crops, carrots and peas are likely to do less well.

WHEN TO DIG

Soil should never be dug when it is very wet or very dry, as this damages soil structure. Autumn is generally recommended as the best time to dig clay soils, when they are more workable. Light soils can be dug at any time during the year, although it is often more convenient to dig in spring. This is when you are most likely to start a raised bed (see pp. 20–5). On clay soils, covering the soil with polythene beforehand (see p. 37) helps to get it into workable condition.

ACID OR ALKALI

The acidity of the soil is known as its pH. A neutral soil has a pH of 7. Acid soils have a pH below 7, and alkaline soils a pH above 7.

Generally speaking, sandy soils tend to be slightly acid and clay soils tend to be neutral or slightly alkaline. The pH of the soil is important because it influences the availability of soil nutrients to the plants, and thus the overall fertility of the soil, and has a bearing on soil life, which affects the general health of the soil. In addition, some crops such as legumes (peas and beans) and brassicas need an alkaline soil, while others do better in slightly acid soils.

The simple way to determine the pH of your soil is to buy a testing kit, which comes with full instructions. A pH of 6.5 – a slightly acid soil – is ideal. This is the pH in which most vegetables do best. As it happens, this is what most British soils tend to be; so although pH is very important, it does not usually present any problems.

Any slight imbalance is readily corrected by the application of lime if the soil is too acid, or organic matter if the soil is alkaline. Lime should not be added with other fertilizers and is usually applied in autumn; but don't be too hasty. Over-liming can cause its own problems. If your soil seems healthy and the worm population is good, then assume everything is fine. If you think you have a severe problem, consult an expert.

FERTILITY

High fertility is essential for successful crops. This is achieved by incorporating lots of organic matter into the soil, supplemented by fertilizers as necessary. Bulky organic matter does not have much plant food but is invaluable as a soil conditioner and humus-former, whereas fertilizers supply the necessary back up to fertility but should be used sparingly. Concentrated organic fertilizers are best for general purposes. Garden compost (see pp. 18–20) is the ideal all-round fertilizer and soil improver.

ORGANIC MATTER

Mention organic matter and the image of barrowloads of muck immediately comes to mind. For small modern gardens, however, there are sweet-smelling alternatives which are readily available from garden centres or through mail order. Spent mushroom compost and forest bark are both very good soil improvers, as are the various proprietary animal manures which have been rotted down ready for use. The function of all of these – as indeed it is with straight farmhouse muck – is to increase the bulk of organic humus-forming matter in the soil, giving it 'body'. This is the first step towards building a healthy, fertile soil and its importance cannot be stressed enough. As I describe on p. 15, it is essential to both sandy and clay soils.

A soil rich in organic matter improves soil structure and drainage, and provides the right environment for a multitude of beneficial soil bacteria and soil organisms, including earthworms. It is these that give soil its life and vitality, which in turn is passed onto the plants and reflects in their overall vigour. How much bulky organic matter you need to include depends on your soil, but my general feeling is you can never have enough. Certainly it should be added until the soil reaches a lovely humus-rich state; this has the feel and appearance of dark chocolate cake and is as easy to dig as it is to slice a cake. Thereafter, dig in as you feel it is necessary.

GENERAL FERTILIZERS

These are concentrated sources of soluble nutrients and their role is to ensure that the plant has what it needs when it needs it. One of the most useful is an all-purpose general organic fertilizer, such as blood, fish and bonemeal, which supplies the three main nutrients, nitrogen, phosphorus and potassium (NPK), in the necessary balanced proportions. I use this as a matter of course before sowing most vegetables. Concentrated organic fertilizers, which look like well-rotted compost or manure, are also very good. These are clean to handle and can be used as a top-dressing throughout the season, or may be dug in just prior to sowing and planting. It is generally better to apply organic matter, manures and fertilizers in spring rather than autumn, otherwise heavy winter rains will wash out many of the soluble nutrients from the soil before the plants need them. Where the use of a specific fertilizer is necessary, caution is generally the best policy – always follow directions as over-use can harm plants.

PLANT NUTRIENTS

Plants need a wide range of nutrients to grow successfully. In gardening-speak, these are divided into 'major' and 'minor' nutrients. Major nutrients are needed in relatively large quantities and are the most important nutrients that every plant needs. Nitrogen, potassium and phosphorus are the three most prominent; calcium and magnesium are also major nutrients. Minor nutrients are known as trace elements and include iron, boron, manganese, zinc, copper and molybdenum. They are only needed in minute quantities by plants but are still vital for healthy growth. One of the best ways to ensure these is to apply seaweed meal, a slow-acting soil conditioner, containing many of the trace elements essential to plants and natural soil flora and fauna.

Lack of any essential nutrients results in recognized deficiency symptoms such as stunted growth or mottled leaves. However, a soil which is managed along organic lines, rich in organic matter and topped up with regular dressings of organic fertilizer, plus seaweed meal, will contain a good balance of all major and minor nutrients. Deficiencies are the exception rather than the rule, so rest assured; and don't be concerned if you see the occasional yellow leaf.

COMPOST

Compost is rotted-down vegetable matter which has broken down into a dark, crumbly, sweet-smelling, friable mass. It costs nothing to make and provides humus, organic matter, and a pot-pourri of essential nutrients and trace elements. A small garden cannot hope to be self-sufficient, but should be able to make enough compost to provide a valuable contribution to garden fertility. For those gardeners who really do find very little vegetable waste, I would advise buying or making a worm compost bin, and making worm compost instead.

You can either make your own compost bin, or buy one of the many purpose-made types now available. These are expensive but durable and will last for many years. A really cheap and easy solution is a tea chest, which can be bought for next to nothing. The size is almost ideal, and each tea chest will last two or three years. All you need to do is to knock out the bottom and the compost bin is ready to use.

Suitable materials include all kitchen vegetable waste and most garden waste (see below). Ideally, a bin of compost should be made in one go, by first chopping and then thoroughly mixing all available compost material, piling it loosely into the bin, and putting a cover on top. One to two weeks later, the contents are then 'turned' to aerate the heap, which is then left to rot. This is the 'hot' method; made this way the heap heats up and rots down very quickly to usable compost in a matter of weeks.

However, in my experience, because compost bins tend to be quite large for the amount of material available at any given time, this is virtually impossible to achieve in small gardens and, generally, compost has to be made in a more piecemeal fashion, filling the bin gradually by adding the material in layers. This is the 'cold' method; the compost takes much longer to make (up to six to twelve months) and the top layers will not be sufficiently decomposed. It also means that 'turning' the compost is not so practical. What I do is wait until I think the compost is usable (dig down and see what the bottom and middle layers look like), then remove the top undecomposed layers, excavate the compost that's ready, and keep it covered separately, then put the top layers back into the bottom of the bin to restart the cycle. The other thing you can do is move the bin to a new spot, covering the half-rotted compost with black plastic or a piece of old carpet and start filling the bin again with new material. The alternative – and a method I am going to try in future – is to make a smaller-sized compost bin (tea chests come in small sizes), one more suited to the amount of material you can find which will enable you to fill the bin in one go.

Both methods work equally well, as long as you follow these basic steps:

● Make sure there is sufficient ventilation and drainage; before putting the bin in place, fork over the ground first to loosen the soil to help with drainage and to allow easy passage of worms into the bin.

● Always roughly chop or tear compost material into smaller pieces and mix well first before adding to the heap. Organic fertilizers, rotted manure, nettles and comfrey are good compost activators and one of these should be added; mix a little in with the rest of the compost material.

● Arrange compost material in neat layers: a depth of 6–9 in (15–23 cm) is ideal; too thin a layer does not work as well and cools down too quickly.

● If you are making compost in a piecemeal fashion, make sure you keep the bin well aerated by forking up the layers as you go along; and never throw in small amounts of kitchen waste or vegetable matter piecemeal but set them aside until you have sufficient to add a proper layer.

● Cover the top of the compost bin; a piece of old carpet is excellent – and the best cheap cover by far.

● Moisture is rarely a problem – but if the heap is very dry, water with a watering can.

● Never use diseased material to make compost; perennial weeds; weeds that have gone to seed; fallen autumn leaves. Brassica stems need to be chopped first (I don't bother putting them in the heap). Clods of earth and tough woody material should also be avoided.

● Do not add thick layers of grass mowings – these quickly rot down to a slimy mess; mix them first thoroughly with other material.

● Leave a layer of compost in the bottom of the bin as a starter for the next heap; these provide a ready source of soil organisms and microbes.

WEEDS

Weeds compete with crops for light, moisture and nutrients, as well as harbouring pests and disease, so they should be removed. Annual weeds are easily dealt with – an onion hoe makes short work of any which do not come out of the ground easily by hand. Pull them up before they flower and put them in the compost bin. They can also be dug into the soil, but make sure you bury them upside down and very deeply, and don't dig in any that have seed heads.

Perennial weeds need to be dug out, for their roots are persistent and even a fraction left in the ground will rapidly produce another new weed. The main offenders are creeping buttercup, bindweed, couch grass, nettles, ground elder and the good old dandelion.

If you need to clear an area, one of the simplest ways to remove annual weeds and grasses is to cover the ground with black polythene (old carpet and cardboard are alternatives but are even less attractive to look at). This starves the weeds of light, gradually killing them off, and takes a couple of months if applied in spring and summer when they are growing rapidly.

Weeds are not all bad news. They give an indication of the fertility of the soil, or its acidity, for example. As well as harbouring pests some also attract beneficial or nice-to-know insects. Stinging nettles are the outstanding example: they indicate a fertile soil, are an excellent compost activator, and provide home to tortoiseshell and peacock butterflies.

PREPARING RAISED VEGETABLE BEDS

Raised beds, or deep beds, are *the* solution for any modern or small garden. If you have never grown vegetables before, I can't think of a better way to start. So, first, exactly what are they?

There is nothing especially magical or mysterious about a 'raised' or 'deep' bed. Nor is this a new idea; the Elizabethans grew vegetables in raised beds and the Chinese have used this method of cultivation for centuries. Either term simply refers to a narrow bed which has been dug to two spits deep (known as double digging) and into

An attractive raised bed, sheltered by a high hedge, neatly edged with wooden planks and surrounded by well-made paths for easy maintenance. The intensively grown crops include beetroot, summer turnips and, in the foreground, flowers help to attract beneficial insects.

which bulky organic matter has been incorporated. The action of digging and the addition of organic matter raises the bed above the level of the surrounding soil, so that each newly finished bed looks rather like a primitive burial mound. Once the bed has been prepared, the soil is never walked on, all work being carried out by reaching inward from the side. The beds are separated by narrow paths.

The beds can be various shapes and sizes. A rectangular shape is the most convenient, but you can choose a triangle, circle, or any odd shape that happens to fit the garden. Remembering you have to walk around the bed to get access from both sides, a length of 12–15 ft (3.6–4.5 m) is about right for a large-sized bed. The width of the bed is governed by how far you can comfortably reach from the edge to the middle, generally around 4 ft (1.25 m) – check first that this is comfortable for you. Should you find yourself with an oddly shaped bed which is much wider in one area, put a stepping stone in the middle of the widest part as a balance.

For neatness and ease of maintenance, the beds should be edged: old roofing tiles, bricks, plastic edging, wooden planks, coping stones and log rolls all make suitable edging. The surrounding paths are also important. Avoid grass paths at all costs – these provide homes for slugs and snails and are extremely awkward to mow. Wood shavings, forest bark, black woven plastic hessian, gravel and paving stones are all suit-

able. Old bricks and assorted cobblestones are fine, although weeds do come through the gaps.

The width of the path needs to be enough to allow you to bend down and work comfortably, and to wheel a wheelbarrow down if needed. The recommended width between beds is 2 ft (60 cm), although you can manage with 18 in (45 cm).

Raised beds have many advantages and it's worth looking at each of them in turn:

● Labour saving: a raised bed is a once-and-for-all bed; once the initial preparation work has been carried out, very little maintenance is needed. Effort is also concentrated into where it matters most – there is no wasted effort digging over a whole vegetable plot only part of which will be covered with crops.

● Space saving: raised beds are very compact. They make maximum use of available space, and can be tailor-made to any length.

● Higher yields from less space: this is another big bonus of raised beds. Because the soil is deeply dug, rich in organic matter and never walked on, drainage is better, the soil warms up more quickly and the roots have a freer run. This enables crops to be grown intensively and much closer together than in conventional plots, producing significantly higher yields.

● Less weeding: because the crops are grown close together, there are far fewer weeds; those that do arise are easily removed.

● Manageable and adaptable: of all the benefits, this is the one I almost find the most appealing. A raised bed makes kitchen gardening manageable and therefore within the reach of everyone. It is easy to protect and cover over, the size of vegetables can be controlled by spacing, rotation is simplified, and maintenance is reduced. One could hardly ask for more.

● Good looks: this is another plus point, and an important one for small gardens where garden design and appearance is crucial to the enjoyment of your garden. A raised bed is always neat and tidy and a pleasure to look at, especially when chock-full of healthy crops. Edging the bed contributes a decorative feature and offers lots of scope for the creatively minded gardener.

MAKING A RAISED BED

Orientation Wherever possible, plan the length of the bed to run north to south. This way, all the plants receive an equal amount of sunshine.

Marking out the bed Mark out the bed with a line or canes, checking the width is comfortable.

Double digging Double digging forms the foundations of the new vegetable plot. As the illustrations on the next page show, it involves digging a trench, loosening the subsoil, adding organic matter and finally filling in the trench with top soil taken from the adjacent spit. Its main function is to improve drainage. Adding organic matter improves soil structure, builds up humus, and increases fertility.

BED MAINTENANCE

During the season, the bed tends to settle and flatten. Each year, to build up humus and keep the soil in tip-top condition, more organic matter needs to be incorporated into the bed, which raises it again. If you only have one bed, this may have to be done in piecemeal fashion; otherwise it is better to do each bed in turn as it becomes vacant. If the bed is not edged it will need to be redefined and the edges tidied up.

The beds are only double dug once, when they are first made. Thereafter, the top spit is dug as necessary until the soil is in good heart.

THE NO-DIG ALTERNATIVE

The conventional method of making a raised bed is to double dig the plot as described above. There is, however, an alternative. The common misconception that soil needs to be dug is not necessarily true (nature doesn't dig, after all) and there are many

DOUBLE DIGGING

1 Dig a trench one spit wide and one spit deep – that is, a spade's width and depth. This is the top spit. Use a wheelbarrow to take the soil to the other end of the bed.

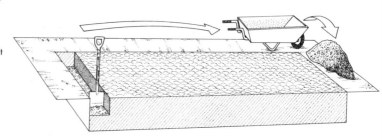

2 Loosen the soil in the bottom of the trench with a fork; work to the depth of the fork if possible. This is the second spit.

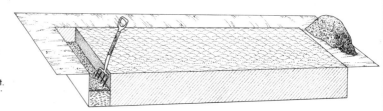

3 Backfill with fresh soil taken from the top spit of the next trench, mixing it well with organic matter.

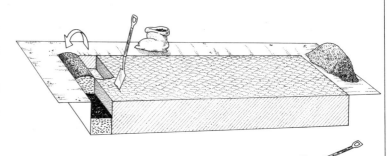

4 Repeat steps 1–3 along the length of the bed. Use the soil from the first spit to fill the last trench. Finally, rake over to produce a smooth even mound.

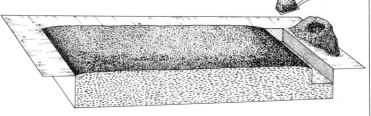

organic gardeners who prefer not to dig the soil, but to mark out and edge the bed as before, pile well rotted organic matter on top to form an organic mulch and grow the crops on this, either in shallow seed drills or transplanting the plants directly into the soil below. This is called the no-dig method of cultivation. To start the bed, instead of removing weeds or turf by digging them out, the area is covered over with black plastic or old carpet until the weeds have died off and the soil is bare. Its main advantages are that it protects the existing soil structure, and does not disturb earthworms and other soil organisms and creatures. These effectively do all the hard work, gradually taking organic matter down into the soil, building up humus and improving fertility. It also produces a friable top soil for successful seed germination and reduces moisture loss.

For people who cannot dig for one reason or another, or for those who would rather not dig, or who may be worried about their backs, provided that the bed is regularly dressed with organic matter, the no-dig system provides an excellent way of cultivating vegetables just as successfully as conventionally dug raised beds. To get the best results, however, like all methods of growing vegetables, there are modifications and practices suited to that particular method. Much depends on individual circumstances.

Speaking as one who has always used the conventionally dug raised-bed system, my feeling is that for new or inexperienced gardeners, unless your soil structure is very good, the dig system is the best one to start with, especially for those small gardens where it is difficult to make enough compost or to get hold of sufficient supplies of well-rotted organic matter. Where drainage is a problem, or on heavy clay soils or compacted soils, I would definitely recommend double digging the bed initially. Once the soil improves sufficiently, digging becomes redundant and the beds are virtually run on a no-dig system anyway.

To help you decide, *Beds* by Pauline Pears (see p. 123) is one of the best practical guides on both dig and no-dig beds.

2

SOWING AND GROWING

The heart of gardening is growing the crops. Everything else a gardener does is to produce the right conditions so that crops grow well, are healthy and, as a consequence, full of flavour. Learning the craft of sowing and planting is essential to success, and is just as important as soil fertility.

STARTING FROM SEED

Most crops are grown from seed. There is a far greater choice of varieties available from seeds than from young plants you can buy, and it prevents any worry about the possibility of introducing pests and diseases. For the majority of vegetables, the easiest way is to sow the seed directly in the soil. Early or tender crops are raised inside, either in seed trays or in individual modules, and planted out when the weather is suitable. This is becoming the standard way to raise many vegetables. For small gardens it makes very good sense, particularly for plants which transplant well or when just a few plants are needed, and has the advantage of greater

flexibility when it comes to planting out.

I would recommend using both methods, mixing and matching to suit your garden needs and conditions as appropriate. Which method you settle on for what crop comes with experience and develops over the years as you settle into a pattern of gardening which works for you. With either, what young plants most need is steady continuous growth and a gentle guiding hand. The golden rule is to avoid any strain or stress on the plants due to adverse growing conditions, be it the weather, rough handling, or forgetting to water them at the right time.

GERMINATION

Seeds require warmth and moisture to germinate. Most germinate in light or dark con-

A vegetable bed in mid-summer showing a range of popular crops grown from seed. Seed is either sown direct or raised inside and planted out when the weather is suitable. Climbing French beans, grown inside in individual pots, are supported by a simple cane wigwam and make excellent use of restricted space in small gardens.

ditions and within a temperature range of 40–50°F (5–10°C) – though different vegetables germinate within different temperature bands, and this obviously affects the time span for sowing in the garden. Generally, the higher the temperature, the faster the germination. Seeds will not germinate unless they have moisture to soften the seed coat and trigger off the germination process. Too much moisture will cause seeds and seedlings to stagnate and rot.

Until a seedling emerges from the soil it has to live off its own food reserves, hence it is important to sow evenly at the right depth for the type of seed. The general rule is to sow seeds at a depth twice their own size. In practice, this simply means all tiny and small seeds should be covered over as lightly as you can manage. Sowing can be slightly deeper on light soils than on heavy soils; larger and more vigorous seeds can be sown more deeply, around ½–1½ in (1.25–3.75 cm), depending on their size.

SUCCESSFUL SOWING OUTSIDE

Two things are critical for sowing seeds successfully outside: soil temperature and soil 'tilth'. To a certain extent these are related – a warm soil is drier and easier to work than a cold one.

TEMPERATURE

Wait until the soil has warmed up (feel it with your hand) before sowing seeds out-side. This means sometime in March or April, or in April or May for colder areas. Weeds also provide a good test for sowing outside in spring – when they start to grow well it is usually warm enough to start sowing. If you do want to sow early, warm the soil beforehand with a protective sheet of polythene and protect the seed beds with horticultural fleece (see pp. 37–8), which also keeps the soil moist and warm. Very large seeds, such as courgette seeds, can be covered with an upturned jam jar or a cut-off plastic bottle (see p. 39), which acts as a mini-cloche.

Some seeds, notably lettuce and parsley, do not germinate well in hot temperatures. You need to cool down the soil, watering well beforehand, sowing early in the day or in shady positions. Compared to spring, soil temperatures are often warmer in autumn, and seeds of overwintered crops often germinate successfully at this time.

TILTH

This refers to the top 1 in (2.5 cm) or so of soil which has been broken down to produce a fine, crumbly surface, without stones or clods of earth. This allows the seeds to make the necessary contact with the water in the pore spaces, which in turn gives the seeds the best chance of good germination. Tiny seeds such as carrots need a fine tilth; larger seeds like peas and beans can cope with a coarser tilth.

The simplest and best way to get the soil

into condition quickly is, again, to cover it with thick polythene a month or so beforehand; so much so, I now wouldn't dream of starting a new season without first covering the vegetable plot in this way.

SOWING DIRECT

There are two methods for sowing direct, sowing the seeds in rows by drawing out narrow V-shaped slits or drills in the soil with a stick or hand fork, then covering the seeds with a thin layer of soil; or broadcasting the seed by scattering it over the surface of the soil and raking it in lightly. Broadcasting is particularly useful for quick crops or catch crops that you harvest young, and where spacing doesn't really matter. For both methods, the soil must be properly prepared by breaking up the clods of earth and raking down to a fine tilth.

Watering the soil should always be done before, not after sowing. The secret is to use the finest rose possible on the can and to water very lightly, just enough to dampen the surface. Imagine a light April shower and get as close as you can to that. In dry conditions, water the drill first. In wet conditions, line the drill with sowing or potting compost; cover the seeds with compost. Sow the seed thinly (small seeds), using just a pinch of seed at a time; larger seeds can be stationed at intervals. The seedbed must be kept damp until the seeds have germinated – water every day in dry weather.

Once the seeds have been covered, the textbook way to finish sowing is to firm the soil gently with the back of a trowel or the back of your hand to ensure good contact with the soil. My husband – whose seeds never fail to germinate – has a slightly different method which certainly works for clay soils. Using a hand fork, merely tickle the surface of the soil next to the drill, so that it moves very slightly across the seeds until they are just covered over. Do not firm or pat down the soil. If the tilth is not as fine as it should be, or when there are very few seeds in a packet, place the seeds on the side of the drill rather than the bottom so that they do not become buried too deeply.

Label each row, showing the date of sowing and the variety.

THINNING OUT

Emerging seedlings soon crowd each other, competing for light and moisture, and generally speaking, must be 'thinned' by pulling out and removing seedlings either side to allow for those that remain to grow on properly. This is usually done progressively, two or three times over a month or so, starting when the seedlings are very small and gradually thinning the young plants to their final spacing. Select the strongest seedlings and thin when the soil is moist, watering first if necessary, and gently firming the soil back around the seedlings if it has been disturbed. Often, young thinnings such as lettuce can be used in salads.

Although common garden practice, it's worth pointing out that some crops – early root vegetables, mini-leeks and small salad plants, for example – will grow very successfully without thinning, and it may be worth experimenting to find out what works best for you.

SOWING INSIDE

Plants can be raised quite happily in clean plastic containers, such as yoghurt pots with drainage holes punched in the bottom. Another cheap and useful idea is to sow into cardboard tubes saved from kitchen and toilet paper rolls. These can be cut and stacked in plastic containers and used as home-made individual modules. It's a good idea generally to sow the seeds in small containers or individual modules big enough to allow the plant to grow on without the bother of pricking out, or having to transplant it into a bigger pot before transplanting outside. It's easier and, most importantly, it means less root disturbance for the plant and therefore less check to growth. Multi-purpose sowing and potting composts are convenient, work well, and have enough nutrients to allow the plant to grow until it is planted outside.

SOWING AND GERMINATION

Sowing and germinating seeds inside is very straightforward. For this stage the quality of light is not important. For proper growth, once the seeds have germinated, the seedlings *must* have full light; this is particularly important at the seed leaf (cotyledon) stage. Beware of very bright windowsills which cause the seedlings to grow weak and spindly.

For seeds which require high germination temperatures and warm conditions to grow well – tomatoes, peppers, cucurbits – a small propagator is best; failing this, a warm airing cupboard usually suffices. It's also a good idea to start them off in the later rather than earlier recommended sowing times.

GROWING ON

To grow on, seedlings need to be given more room. Thin them soon after they germinate, to leave just a few, and space them evenly apart. Once two or three proper leaves have formed, remove all but the strongest seedlings and leave to grow on until ready to transplant or to pot on further.

POTTING ON

Potting on means moving a plant which has outgrown its container into a larger pot. If you wait until the plant becomes 'pot-bound', which means it has outgrown its space and food supply, you may stunt the plant's subsequent development forever. It's applicable mainly to tender plants such as tomatoes, peppers and cucurbits, which need both warmth and a long growing season, but the same principle applies to any plant started off inside that you need to keep

SOWING AND GERMINATION

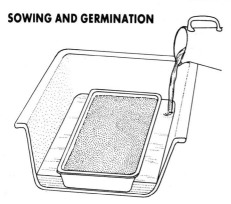

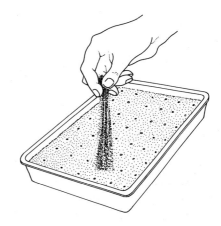

1 Fill the container loosely to ½ in (1.2 cm) from the top with sowing and potting compost and firm the surface very gently with something flat. Stand the container in a bowl of shallow water until thoroughly damp. Lift out and allow excess water to drain away from the bottom.

2 Sow the seeds on the surface, spacing thinly. Cover with a thin layer of compost; leave very small seeds uncovered.

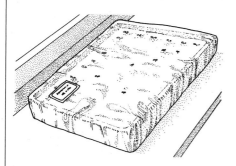

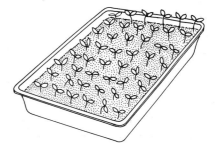

3 Cover the container with clear glass, a plastic bag or clingfilm, (or dark polythene if dark conditions are necessary for germination). This is to keep the seeds moist, as dry seeds will not germinate. In strong sunlight, cover with a sheet of newspaper. Label the container and put it somewhere warm and of an even temperature – a suitable windowsill or conservatory, for instance.

4 Check regularly, removing the plastic covering immediately the seeds have germinated, generally around four to ten days after sowing. From now on, move to good light, but not hot, bright sunlight, and an airy position (not a steamy kitchen). Keep the compost moist but not waterlogged; water from the base, letting the container drain thoroughly as above.

POTTING ON

1 Pot on the plant when the roots start to poke out the bottom of its existing container.

2 Fill the new pot three-quarters full of compost, then press in the old pot with the plant still intact. This gives an imprint of the exact amount of space the root ball will fill.

3 Tap the bottom of the pot and invert to remove the plant, cradling it carefully between the fingers. Ease it out gently; never hold plants by the stem, especially very young plants.

4 Insert into the new pot, situating the bottom of the stem about 1 in (2.5 cm) below the top. Backfill with new compost, firming gently. Tap the top to settle the compost. Water from the bottom and keep out of direct sunlight until re-established.

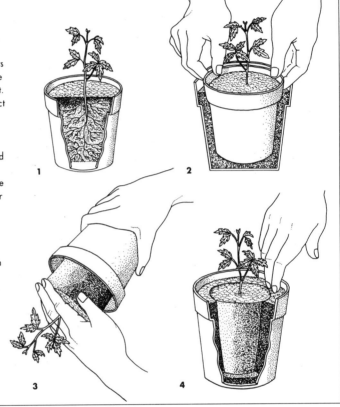

'on hold' before it can be planted outside or into its final container.

HARDENING OFF

Hardening off is the term used to describe acclimatizing plants raised inside for their more precarious life outside. It ensures the plants continue to grow smoothly without stress or check. As soon as the roots are starting to fill their containers, the plants should be prepared for transplanting. The important thing is to get plants used to the cold at night.

Stand the plants outside for a few days (presuming the weather is suitable), bringing them in at night. Then leave them out at night as well, in a sheltered spot, covering them first with horticultural fleece (see pp. 37–8) before finally removing the fleece at night as well. Alternatively, plants can be put out under a cloche or hardened off in a cold frame, (see p. 39) gradually exposing the plant to daytime and night-time temperatures.

TRANSPLANTING

Transplanting is probably the biggest shock plants will encounter in their lives. The golden rule is to minimize root disturbance as much as possible. When you think that uprooting plants from a seed tray or bed causes 25–50 per cent root damage, it's easy to see the advantage of individually raised plants which are transplanted with their roots more or less intact. Within reason, the younger the plant the better it will transplant and the sooner it will recover.

In poor or heavy soils, mix the compost, peat or coir (see p. 110) into the transplanting hole. Avoid planting out in hot weather; in summer, transplant in the early morning or evening. Once transplanted, keep well watered, watering around the base of the plant until it is re-established.

STORING SEEDS

Gardeners with small gardens rarely need a whole packet of seed. Knowing which seeds can be kept and give reliable results next season is not just comforting, it can make an appreciable difference to the hole in your pocket.

It is not generally appreciated that no batch of seeds will ever give 100 per cent germination. Broadly speaking, flat seeds do not germinate as well as round seeds. The longer the seeds are stored, the fewer will germinate; of those that do, often the plants do not grow as well, and have less 'vigour' than plants from fresh seed.

Most seeds can be happily kept until the next season. Most seeds can also be stored for two or three seasons and still give reliable results. If you want to extend it further, brassicas can be kept for about four years, and cucurbits (cucumbers, marrows and squashes) and tomatoes about six years, though it should be stressed that the seed has to be stored properly and it is always wise to germinate a sample of old seed first, to see if the germination rate is still acceptable.

I buy seed every two to three years, except parsley seed, which should be bought fresh every year.

Nothing ages seeds faster than warmth or destroys them quicker than moisture. The best place to store seeds is actually the refrigerator, though I hardly think this is a practical suggestion for the majority of households, certainly not mine! In practice, we must do the best we can: store seeds, wrapped in their packets, in airtight, moisture-proof containers – glass preserving jars are ideal – and keep in the coolest (not damp) room available. The temperature should be even and not fluctuate; the kitchen or garden shed is not suitable. Foil-wrapped seeds last longer while unopened, but deteriorate faster once exposed to the air.

BUYING PLANTS

For small gardens, there are occasions when it makes sense to buy plants rather than raise them yourself. It saves labour and is not necessarily more expensive. Suitable candidates include plants that you only need one or two of, such as perennial herbs; crops that you need in very small quantities, such as some annual herbs; and those which are tender, such as French beans, peppers or courgettes – though with these the choice of variety will be restricted, so check first that it is one you are happy to grow.

In every case, only buy sturdy, healthy plants that look in tip-top condition: examine the leaves and general vigour of the plant. If it is leggy or looks weak, or is pale, or has outgrown its pot, or is in dire need of water, avoid it.

SPACING CROPS

All crops need space to grow, providing the necessary air, light and moisture – literally giving the plants room to breathe. But there is probably more conflicting advice on exactly how much space you need to leave between each plant than on anything else in gardening books. Gardening in rows is no more than an accident of agricultural history, dating back to the seventeenth century when Jethro Tull invented the seed drill and a hoe which horses could pull to do the weeding. The seed drill meant seed was no longer broadcast, but sown in rows; and the hoe meant there had to be sufficient space between the rows for the horses to get through. One of the most welcome developments in recent years has been the realization that vegetables can be grown closer together and give just as reliable, sometimes better, results. This is good news for small gardens and means that you *can* garden intensively with confidence.

For small gardens and modern families, being able to produce smaller-sized vegetables by growing them closer together than traditional spacings is often a positive bonus. As every garden has slightly different conditions, it's worth while experimenting to find out which spacings suit yours best. I am a big believer, for example, in plants being 'comfortable' and a rule of thumb I find increasingly useful is to think

The Cook's Garden, created from an existing herbaceous border measuring 20 x 4 ft (6 x 1.2 m), showing a variety of small salad plants (land cress, rocket and lamb's lettuce) and salad bowl lettuce being grown closely together. In the background are mature fennel and young Swiss chard plants. A tub of flowering nasturtiums encourages beneficial insects and provides edible leaves for salads.

about the final size of the vegetable or the area it will occupy; allow a bit for elbow room, and that's the spacing to aim for. This seems to work well for all low-growing plants. For tall plants which cast long shadows you need to allow for increased competition for light; but even so, if you use common sense and think about the final size of the vegetable, you can usually make a reasonable guess at how much space to leave.

On raised beds crops are always grown close together, either in short rows across the bed, or in some 'staggered' form of layout so that crops are grown in blocks. Staggering the crops allows maximum use of the ground and there is less competition for light between the plants. In practice, one tends to use both methods (I still like rows), depending on the crop and size of the plant, and whether the crops are sown direct or transplanted. What works for you on your soil is what counts every time. Throughout the book I have given the general spacings that I use, which should be suitable in most cases.

CROP ROTATION

Crop rotation is a traditional garden practice which involves taking care not to grow certain groups of vegetables in the same spot every year. They are moved in sequence around the plot so that they do not return to the same position for three to four years. Rotation is practised for three reasons: firstly as a safeguard to help prevent build-up of pests and disease; secondly, to make better use of the plant foods in the soil, as different crops use up different nutrients; and thirdly, to make crop management easier as each group has different requirements – for instance, brassicas need lime.

For cultural purposes, vegetables are divided into three broad groups and 'rotated' as follows: legumes, brassicas and roots.

● Legumes: roots manufacture nitrogen which improves soil fertility.

● Brassicas: need lime and benefit from the nitrogen left by legumes. They loosen the soil.

● Roots: Should not be grown on recently manured soil and like loose soil, so follow brassicas.

For small gardens, where vegetables are often grown in one small bed, or mixed in with the ornamental garden, crop rotation is usually impractical and far less relevant. Nevertheless the general principles apply: keep the basic groups and vegetable families in mind when planning the layout of the bed and don't grow crops from the same botanical family in the same piece of ground two years running. Finally, keep a note of where you planted each group – even with the best intentions, it's surprising how such things can slip your mind.

MAJOR BOTANICAL FAMILIES

The vegetables listed in this book belong to the following families:

Alliaceae: onion, shallot, leek, garlic, Welsh onion, spring onion

Chenopodiaceae: beetroot, spinach, spinach beet, chard

Compositae: lettuce, chicory, endive

Cruciferae: brassicas – cabbage, kale, kohl rabi, sprouting broccoli, turnip. Also, cress, radish, rocket

Cucurbitaceae: courgettes, squashes, cucumbers

Leguminosae: peas and beans

Umbelliferae: carrots, Hamburg parsley. Also, dill, chervil.

PROTECTING THE CROPS

For small gardens, where every single carrot counts, giving the crops the best start is crucial to success. Protecting the crops plays a major role here. By protection, gardeners mean giving the crops shelter of some kind, primarily from wind and cold, by means of cloches and other protective coverings which create their own warm micro-environment. The two vital periods when crops most benefit from protection are when they are young, and during the very cold months of the year.

To protect crops successfully, it's not necessary to have a greenhouse or walk-in polythene tunnel. Much can be achieved by a judicious combination of protective materials and a few cloches (even makeshift ones) or a simple cold frame. Don't forget that in summer these coverings can quickly become baking hot and airless – so don't be too enthusiastic about protecting crops unless they need it.

POLYTHENE

The prime value of this material is in covering the bed in late winter or early spring, to keep off excessive rain and to warm up the soil in readiness for sowing (see p. 28). For this, thick polythene is best – any kind will do, though black polythene is preferable as it inhibits weed growth and warms up the soil slightly sooner than clear plastic. As a protective covering for young crops, however, it is nothing like as good as the horticultural fleece described next; condensation is a major problem with polythene, and slugs collect underneath.

HORTICULTURAL FLEECE

For small gardens this is the perfect all-purpose protective medium, not the cheapest but worth every penny, especially if you garden in a cold area. It looks like a flimsy white shroud and acts like a floating cloche, except that in many ways it is even better. It lets in air, light and moisture, and provides crops with excellent protection from cold and wind. It can be applied at any time during the growing season and can be left on if necessary until crops reach maturity – being light, it simply rises as the crops grow, which they do wonderfully well under fleece. It also guards against carrot fly and other pests and keeps cats at bay. It is stronger than it appears, and should last three or more seasons if handled properly. Take care not to tear it, and not to lift it before removing any stones used to weight it down – and keep well clear with the strimmer!

Fleece is most valuable in the early part of the growing season – spring and early summer – and again in autumn. It is not strong enough to withstand winter weather, piles of snow and strong winds. Conversely, in hot weather, crops can swelter under its protective shell and it is best to remove it.

CLOCHES

There are many different kinds of cloches and there is no doubting their usefulness. I would recommend investing in at least two. Whereas horticultural fleece is best for protecting a whole bed or sizeable area, cloches can be used to protect individual plants or short rows, and can be moved easily from one place to another.

Generally speaking, you get what you pay for. Cheap plastic cloches do not last well, are often not very sturdy, may blow away easily and are sometimes fiddly to use, but do the job and should last a couple of seasons at least. Glass cloches, by contrast, are heavy and – as anyone who has them knows – the glass panels inevitably break from time to time, which can be dangerous where there are children in the garden. Small cloches and low polythene tunnels can become overheated and suffer badly from condensation. For these reasons, I would advise choosing the largest and sturdiest cloche that is likely to suit your needs. I find that the best are barn-style cloches reaching about 12 in (30 cm) high at the centre. These are large and airy enough to place over sizeable as well as small plants, and

A large, polythene-covered, lightweight barn cloche is easily manoeuvred and covers the width of the raised bed affording maximum protection to young endive plants and lettuce. Ventilation holes allow air to circulate freely and prevent condensation.

have handles for easy movement. Larger cloches also provide better air circulation with less risk of build-up of pests and disease. Make sure the cloches fit the width of your bed, either singly or by putting two cloches together.

For the resourceful gardener or DIY enthusiast, home-made cloches provide a cheaper alternative. Large plastic water bottles with their ends cut off and plastic caps removed make excellent mini-cloches for young plants (If you ever get round to having an asparagus bed, they are perfect for protecting individual spears.) Only cut off the base of the bottle – this gives you lots of length to ram into the soil for anchorage. Condensation builds up quickly and you should check that leaves do not touch the wet plastic, as this may cause rotting.

Cloches have many uses and will repay the outlay many times. Using them extends the season by two to three weeks at either end of the year. In spring they can be used for early crops and hardening off; in summer for protecting tender crops; in autumn for late sowings of salad crops; and in winter for protecting autumn-sown garlic and all salad plants. They keep animals away and are handy for ripening onions, or to pop over parsley, chervil or mint in early spring to bring them on.

COLD FRAMES

A cold frame is a simple four-sided box with a hinged or sliding glass or plastic top,

known as the 'light'. Depending on what you want the frame for, it may or may not have soil in the bottom. Think of it either as a huge square or rectangular cloche or an unheated mini-greenhouse. It is used to grow early crops such as salad plants and early carrots; to grow on young plants in a protected environment when they are very young; to overwinter cuttings and salad plants; and to harden plants off. For small gardens, a frame is invaluable as it performs the same role as a greenhouse but takes up far less space and is far less expensive.

For growing vegetables you will need a sizeable frame, and you should consider its depth carefully. A clearance of about 9–12 in (23–30 cm), for example, is fine for low-growing salad plants; but for taller plants like bush tomatoes, a clearance height of 18 in (45 cm) or more is necessary. It is important that the lights can be moved easily and open fully – as with cloches, a damp, stagnant atmosphere due to lack of sufficient ventilation can soon cause fungal problems.

WATERING

Heavy-handed watering causes more harm than good to both soil structure and young plants. Always water gently but thoroughly, using a fine rose turned upwards for seedlings. With larger plants, direct the water to the base of the plant (see below). With very large or thirsty plants, such as courgettes, sink a pot into the soil near the plant and direct the water into the pot, which allows it to seep slowly through to the roots.

A good soak every now and then is far more beneficial than water little and often; apply at least 1 in (2.5 cm) of water (check the soil by seeing how far the water has penetrated). Sprinklers can damage surface structure so should not be used too often. The two critical times are sowing and transplanting (see pp. 29 and 33), and when plants are flowering and fruiting. This is especially important for peas and beans, tomatoes and cucurbits; it produces better crops and higher yields. In periods of drought, or if you can only water once, the best time to water is between ten days and three weeks before maturity.

SUCCESSFUL WATER MANAGEMENT

● Dig in plenty of organic matter to improve the water-retaining capacity of the soil.

● Keep the vegetables weed free: weeds steal moisture from the soil.

● Mulch crops if necessary around the plants; put the mulch on after watering or following rainfall, not before. In exposed situations, erect a windbreak or protect with horticultural fleece (see pp. 37-8).

● Water at 'moisture-sensitive' stages of growth: sowing and planting; flowering and fruiting.

● Limit the frequency of watering to when it really counts.

● Water the plants, not the whole bed, trickle water from a hose.

PESTS AND DISEASES

The problem with writing about pests and diseases in the kitchen garden is that it is likely to give an unfavourable impression – especially if you have never grown vegetables before. Rest assured, for most of the time, the majority of vegetables suffer neither pests nor diseases; or if they do, they are not a major problem and the plants recover without too much harm being done.

Particular pests and remedies that affect certain crops are covered where applicable under the appropriate plant entry. The two most common pests, slugs (and snails) and aphids, are discussed below. It's also important always to remember that a problem for one garden is not a problem for all gardens – we all win a few and lose a few – and that prevention is better than cure. The following are a few simple rules and observations that can help enormously.

● Healthy plants always withstand attack better than poorly grown, sickly specimens. A healthy soil breeds healthy plants. You can also ensure healthy plants by keeping them growing continuously and not subject them to stress.

● Encourage beneficial insects which feed on aphids, such as ladybirds, lace wings and hoverflies, by growing flowers and herbs in close proximity to the kitchen garden. This is another benefit of growing vegetables in small gardens – the flowers are never far away. Poached-egg plant, the dwarf convolvulus and French and English marigolds are all excellent for this purpose.

● A dirty garden harbours pests and diseases. One full of weeds means competition with the crops for valuable light, moisture and nutrients, weakening the plants. Weeds also harbour pests and disease.

● Be on the look out for resistant varieties in seed catalogues and grow these where applicable, or if you have had a particular problem with diseased plants.

● Try not to grow the same crops in the same patch twice. This will help towards avoiding build up of particular pests and diseases. (See advice on crop rotation on p. 36.)

● Protecting crops with various physical barriers is an enormous help and the ideal multi-purpose remedy for small gardens where the scale of things generally and the quantity of crops is so much more modest. Similarly, removing pests by hand is often the most effective way of getting on top of pests early.

SLUGS

Slugs (and snails) are among the commonest and most successful pests, eating and burrowing their way through just about anything. They are a particular problem in wet clay soils and exposed gardens. On sandy or dry soils they are rarely a major problem. Their eggs may be laid in the soil at any time and look like tiny transparent globules, usually found in clusters. Look out for these and destroy them whenever you find them.

General good husbandry helps. If at all possible do not have grass paths between the beds for they harbour slugs like nothing else. Gravel or stone will protect the beds more, as slugs do not like crawling over hot, dry stones. Slugs also collect under rotting debris, so keeping the beds clean gives them one less place to hide. Store root crops inside rather than leave them in the ground.

Frogs, hedgehogs and the large ground black beetle are the main natural predators of slugs. They do help; though if you are fortunate enough to have a hedgehog or friendly frog in the vicinity, you cannot use chemical controls because these are harmful.

Physical controls As yet, there is no single safe, simple organic remedy for slug control, which makes a slug problem even more heartbreaking, especially when you are growing small quantities of crops. Preventive measures can be taken and, depending on your slug population, all work to a greater or lesser extent. The following are the most reliable.

● Plastic bottle mini-cloches: (see p. 39). These are probably the most effective and cheapest method of slug control available. Use for protecting young plants.

● Carpet traps: Slugs will collect under pieces of carpet and can be picked off and destroyed. This is better, I find, than the setting out saucers or traps with milk or beer in them, which the cat tends to knock over, and which need constant replenishing. But the carpet trap method only works well if you check and remove the slugs every day – otherwise they crawl out from under the carpet and onto the crops.

● Slugs are most active at night, or early in the morning. Regular forays with a torch help to keep down the numbers.

Chemical controls The main chemical control is slug pellets. These contain metaldehyde and are scattered around the plants. They are very effective, but to be used sparingly. Remove the affected slugs immediately. Aluminium sulphate, sold under various brand names, is another chemical control, available in granules or as a mixture. It is watered over the ground in advance of planting to keep down slug numbers and eggs. Unlike slug pellets, it is rela-

tively safe to other forms of wildlife. Some people find it very effective, though I have had little success.

● Slug tape: This is a thin paper tape impregnated with metaldehyde, laid down to surround the crops on the ground and kept in place with small stones. The slugs eat the tape, leaving the crops. It is very useful for odd plants, or a small patch of seedlings.

APHIDS

Aphids are the other most common pest. They are a diverse group of tiny soft-bodied insects, visible to the eye, usually described as 'greenfly', though they can be a range of colours from white to black. Some, such as the mealy cabbage aphid, are very specific; others colonize a variety of plants and crops. They feed on soft sappy growth, weakening the plant and causing general decline, and live in fast growing colonies, so that one day a leaf may have only a few aphids but the next day it will be encrusted with them. Many secrete a sticky substance, honeydew, which then becomes covered with a sooty mould; while this is not harmful in itself it stops the light from getting to the leaf which stunts plant growth and is disfiguring.

Some aphid species protect themselves by making the leaves curl tightly, or by living under a woolly coating. They overwinter usually as eggs, though in mild winters some adult aphids can be seen, for example, on plants in the greenhouse or indoors. They tend to come in flushes, from spring onwards.

Remedies Aphids have many natural predators, the most important of which are ladybirds, hoverflies and the tiny parasitic wasps *Aphidius*, all of which eat prodigious quantities of aphids. Ladybirds and hoverflies, which look similar to wasps but hover and do not sting, are easily recognized; ladybird larvae, which look like small slate-blue coloured grubs, also eat aphids, and should not be mistaken for a pest. The parasitic wasps have dark bodies and long wings. They are just visible to the naked eye and can usually be found crawling over a thick infestation of aphids. Another indication is the presence of grey-white aphid 'shells' among the live colony of aphids. These are the remains of aphids which have themselves been eaten by young parasitic wasps; the wasps have hatched and grown inside them, emerging from the dead aphids when ready.

Natural predators are a very effective control of aphids, so it is important to encourage them rather than destroy the natural balance by harming them. The problem is that often it takes time for the predator to outstrip the aphids effectively – meantime the aphids have the upper hand.

A few aphids, or a mild attack, are not a severe problem. They are easily wiped off and squashed with the fingers, or you can pick off infected leaf – this is the method I use, and it's quick, effective and harmless. For more persistent attacks, which can be very debilitating for the crops, the aphids can either be sprayed with derris, insecticidal soap, or with a specific aphicide which only kills aphids; a strong jet of water to flush off the colonies also helps control numbers. Remember that insecticidal soap and derris are harmful to predators. Always spray in the evening when the natural predators are least active.

BIRDS AND CATS

Both of these have annoying habits which can cause damage to crops. Birds peck out the tops of shallots, take seedling crops of lettuce, beetroot and spinach, and are very fond of pea flowers. Pigeons can ravage brassicas. Protect the crops with a physical deterrent of some kind, such as horticultural fleece, twine or bird scarers.

Cats are different. To begin with, your own cat is never a problem, only neighbouring cats. They invade the garden and scratch the soil, especially freshly prepared seedbeds, digging up seedlings and young crops in the process as well as leaving their droppings behind. Covering the crops with horticultural fleece or cloches is the only effective solution. Chicken wire barriers work well, but are not particularly attractive and are fiddly to erect. Cat deterrents rarely seem to help.

3

VEGETABLES

The vegetables recommended here can all be grown reliably in a restricted space, and are straightforward to grow. Each particular entry should be used in conjunction with Getting Started (p. 10) and Sowing and Growing (p. 26), which contain detailed advice on growing techniques. Remember that intensively grown vegetables need high fertility. To ensure this, rake in a top dressing of blood, fish and bonemeal or organic fertilizer before sowing the crops.

MINI-VEGETABLES

Mini-vegetables are vegetables grown very close together and harvested when very small. They are the latest development in commercial horticulture and have recently arrived in the shops. Dobies seed merchants (see p. 123) produce the most comprehensive range, selecting specially suited varieties. The range includes beetroot, carrot, courgette, kohl rabi, leek and turnip. Because the vegetables are used when so small, they are harvested sooner, another

potential advantage for small gardens. I have been impressed with those I have tried so far – but what really counts with home-grown vegetables is flavour, so be prepared to let the vegetables grow a little larger by giving them a bit more space than recommended, or leaving them a little longer.

HARVESTING VEGETABLES

Learning to recognize when vegetables are in their prime, how long they remain in good condition on the plant, and what is the best method of keeping them fresh, is one of the most important skills any gardener can have and of paramount importance for small gardens with modest yields. It's also one of the most rewarding aspects of gardening, for it is the best way to really get to know and understand your vegetables. The exact time when each vegetable reaches its peak

A colourful display of vegetables in their prime grown intensively on raised beds and ready for harvesting. Among the vegetables featured are beetroot, cabbages and leeks.

changes from year to year and is dependent on soil, variety, seasonal variation, sowing times, and so on. How long a particular vegetable remains in perfect condition also varies. Most importantly, how *you* like them and what tastes best to *you* are what counts.

Young vegetables are invariably tender, but the common notion of the younger the better is a fallacy. A baby vegetable often has hardly any flavour; speaking personally, I can't see the point, and much prefer to wait a little longer until the flavour has come through. Conversely, once mature, sooner or later all vegetables start to deteriorate, and a kind of creeping senility sets in. Almost as if by sixth sense, this is when slugs, insects and moulds move in. Watch out for this. If the first rule of harvesting is to be aware of when vegetables are at their best, the second is that when a vegetable begins to show its age, you must bring it in and store it inside rather than let it deteriorate further. Most vegetables, if you pick and store them properly, keep perfectly well for several days.

RAW VEGETABLES

Although most vegetables are eaten cooked, one of the best ways to enjoy fresh garden vegetables is to eat them raw. They are crunchy and appetizing and often this is how their superiority and extra sweetness can be appreciated most.

It's also the best way nutritionally, for as soon as you cook vegetables, no matter how carefully, there is some loss of valuable vitamins and minerals. Latest evidence shows that vegetables have an important role in protecting against degenerative diseases such as cancer, and help to keep us feeling young and healthy. As well as providing vitamins, minerals and bio-active substances we need for health, vegetables are rich in anti-oxidants which protect the body against attack. Beta-carotene, which is responsible for the bright colour of carrots, beetroot and tomatoes, and vitamin C, are especially important. Dark green vegetables – spinach, cabbage, watercress, peas, broccolis – contain both and are very beneficial. The golden rule is little and often, and to eat as wide a variety as possible, whatever is best in the garden at the time. When you do cook them, cook them briefly.

The onion family

The onion tribe (*Allium* species) includes onions, shallots, garlic, leeks, chives, long thin onions such as spring onions, the perennial Welsh onion and Japanese bunching onions. None are difficult to grow, but for a small garden there seems little point in growing onions or winter leeks. I would concentrate instead on shallots, garlic and some of the spring onion types, which have a fresh, often milder onion flavour. All succeed best in rich, friable soils, although the spring onion types will grow just about anywhere.

SHALLOTS

Shallots (*Allium cepa*) are small, round or flat-sided, extra sweet, mild-tasting members of the onion family. They grow in clumps from a single bulb, radiating like the points of a star, each bulb producing six to eight mature shallots. They are an ideal crop for small gardens, faster-growing than onions and generally keeping better. They

are expensive to buy and difficult to find, yet are more convenient in size, perfect to use in salads and cooking.

Cultivation: Shallots are grown from sets (immature bulbs) in the same way as onions. A fertile, well-drained, light, firm soil in a sunny position is best. Plant the individual sets as soon as the weather is suitable from late January to early March, 6 in (15 cm) apart in staggered rows, allowing 6–8 in (15–20 cm) between the rows. Push the set firmly into the soil, leaving just the neck showing. Birds tweaking out the necks can be a nuisance; cover with cloches for a month or so until the shallots are growing well. Keep free of weeds (but do not use a hoe, as the roots are close to the surface), and apply a dressing of blood, fish and bonemeal in late spring. They grow to around 9 in (23 cm) tall and wide, and take about five months to mature. Two rows sufficient.

Recommended varieties: 'Topper'.

Harvesting and culinary uses: Harvest when the tops have flopped over and gone brown, in mid-summer. Do not leave them in the ground if conditions are wet. Lift the whole crop, spread out to dry thoroughly for one to two weeks (inside on a sunny windowsill if the weather is unsuitable). To clean, rub off bits of dried skin, and remove the dead stems, then store in trays or netting. Shallots are excellent roasted in their skins in the oven or on the barbecue, or peeled and cooked gently in a covered pan, with butter and a little sugar, to serve with roast meat.

GARLIC

Contrary to popular opinion, garlic (*Allium sativum*) is extremely hardy and easy to grow and an ideal crop for small gardens – I have been growing it successfully for 15 years now without any problems. It may not provide cloves as large as those you can bring home from France but is juicier and better than most you will buy. For small gardens, the best idea is to buy a couple of garlic bulbs from the greengrocer. Choose plump, firm, healthy bulbs with fat cloves. Thereafter save your own bulbs for replanting.

Cultivation: The secret to growing good garlic is to plant it in late autumn, October to early November, rather than in spring. This gives the plant a good start and ensures that it receives the necessary period of cold that garlic needs in its early development for proper formation of the cloves. That said, you can usually get away with planting in February. It needs a rich, well-drained soil and a sunny, sheltered position.

Separate the individual cloves, inserting each one into the soil pointed end up, 1–2 in (2.5–5 cm) deep and 4 in (10 cm) apart, with 9 in (23 cm) between the rows. Cover with cloches – this keeps off the snow and

rain and enables the garlic to get off to a flying start in spring; remove the cloches in late spring when the weather is warm. The shoots may take several weeks to appear. Keep free of weeds during the growing season. The stems reach up to 2 ft (60 cm) tall; a well grown bulb 2–3 in (5–7.5 cm) in thickness. Each row should yield around 10 bulbs. One row sufficient; two to four rows ample, depending on requirements.

Harvesting and culinary uses: Freshly harvested garlic is a wonderful vegetable in its own right. The cloves are plump and juicy, and are sweeter, less pungent and more digestible, raw or cooked, than when garlic has been dried for storage. The crop matures sometime in July to early August. Wait until the tops have started to yellow, and pull up a bulb to see if the cloves are well formed. If not, leave for a week or so longer. Don't leave them too long in wet weather, as this causes the bulbs to rot more quickly. Whole cloves or bulbs are delicious roasted, or added to pot roasts. Garlic purée can be used to flavour soups, sauces or vegetable purées, or can be spread on baked bread.

Drying and storing: To keep garlic any length of time, it must be dried in the same way as you dry shallots (see p. 47). It's easier to clean them first – remove the outer layers of skin – then lay the bulbs out with their tops still intact in a dry, shady spot for one to two weeks, bringing them inside if it rains. Set aside any which are damaged or show signs of rotting around the neck, to use first, trim the roots and remove any rotting foliage. Either braid the bulbs or simply tie them up by their necks and hang in a well-ventilated place for another two weeks to dry out further. Select the best for replanting in late autumn. Never store garlic in a steamy kitchen. Keep it somewhere cool and dark; dried and stored properly, it should remain in good condition for about six months.

The best way to use up old garlic which has begun to sprout is to plant the cloves out in an odd corner of the garden in early spring, or pot them up inside and place on the kitchen windowsill. They produce long green shoots that have a fresh, mild garlic flavour and can be used like chives (see pp. 96–7).

MINI-LEEKS

Mini-leeks (*Allium ampeloprasum* var. *porrum*) are leeks grown specifically to be pulled young over the summer. They are expensive to buy yet easy enough to grow, and take up little space. Any you do not pull can be left to grow on as normal-sized leeks for use in autumn. You must make sure you grow varieties with long white shanks, such as 'King Richard', rather than the standard squat, fat Musselburgh types.

Leeks are the finest tasting of the onion tribe, with a sweeter, gentler and more refined flavour. Mini leeks are especially tender.

Cultivation: Leeks like a rich, friable soil; they do very well on deep beds and improve the soil structure. They are very slow growers in the early stages, so don't worry if they don't make much progress at first. Sow inside in early February, in blocks in deep pots or plastic trays. Thin to ½ in (1.2 cm) apart. When the weather is suitable, sometime in late spring, plant out deeply in clumps using a trowel, watering the hole well first. The secret to a good leek of whatever size is to encourage a good length of

white, so make sure the leeks are well set into the ground. Growing them in blocks also helps them to self-blanch.

Inside sowings will give you mini-leeks from the end of June onwards. Outside sowings should be made from March to May, to give you mini-leeks for pulling from mid to late summer onwards. Sow the seeds fairly thickly in a shallow drill 3–4 in (7.5–10 cm) wide, thinning as before. When you sow, allow 3–4 in (7.5–10 cm) of soil either side of the drill and draw up the soil around the plants as they grow to encourage long whiter shanks. Keep the plants well watered throughout. Mini-leeks grow from 12–24 in (30–60 cm) tall and take around 16–18 weeks to mature to a usable size. One row sufficient.

Recommended varieties: 'King Richard', 'Early Market'.

Harvesting and culinary uses: The recommended size for pulling mini-leeks is the thickness of a pencil. I think this is too thin – they are fiddly to prepare and too slender to be of any real use – and I prefer to pull them when they are about ¾ in (18 mm) thick. Use as ordinary leeks; they are lovely cooked with peas and broad beans, or in any braised summer vegetable dish. They are also delicious served cold as a salad, dressed with a mustard vinaigrette; or dipped in a light batter and deep-fried for one or two minutes.

SPRING ONIONS

It's always handy to have a few spring onions (*Allium cepa*) in the garden, as you can harvest them throughout summer and they are versatile flavouring for cold and cooked dishes.

Cultivation: Sow in shallow drills 1 in (2.5 cm) wide, or in a small patch, broadcasting the seed fairly thickly, any time from March to the end of June. They take 10–12 weeks to mature. No thinning is required; if you leave them, they grow quite large (12 in/30 cm tall) and are still good at the end of the summer. One or two rows sufficient.

Recommended varieties: 'White Lisbon'.

Harvesting and culinary uses: Spring onions can be pulled as needed and used in salads, eaten whole or thinly sliced to mix with rice and tomato salads. Shredded spring onions, green and white, are excellent in stir-fries, to add to clear soups, and cooked with fresh peas and summer carrots.

WELSH ONION

These have nothing to do with Wales and are also known as bunching onions (*Allium fistulosum*). They grow in a bushy clump like chives, producing long, thin onions similar to spring onions. They are perennial and very hardy, an extremely useful onion to have in autumn and winter.

Cultivation: Buy a clump from a herb or garden centre and plant out in ordinary garden soil. They grow to around 9 in (23 cm) tall, spreading outwards and make a useful edging plant or for any odd corner. Divide the clumps when they get too big.

Cultivation: As for spring onions, sowing the seed quite thickly in March to April. Leave to grow, pulling as required once they reach the size of spring onions. By autumn, they will be 1 in (2.5 cm) thick and can grow up to 18 in (45 cm) tall. They survive a mild frost but are not as hardy as Welsh onions.

Recommended varieties:
'Ishikura', 'Hikari'.

Harvesting and culinary uses: As for spring onions.

Recommended varieties: No varieties are specified; sold as 'Welsh onion'.

Harvesting and culinary uses: The white bulb forms just beneath the surface; cut with a sharp knife, leaving the roots in the soil to regrow. Use as you would spring onions.

JAPANESE ONION

These are Japanese varieties of Welsh onion (*Allium fistulosum*), but larger and milder, more like a leek than an onion.

Leafy green vegetables

The three main leafy green vegetables are spinach, spinach beet and Swiss chard. By growing each of them in turn, it's possible to have a spinach-type vegetable virtually all year round. All are easy to grow, free from pests and diseases, and highly nutritious.

For sheer versatility, Swiss chard is probably my favourite dark green vegetable. Spinach beet is a valuable crop for autumn to spring. Summer spinach is less suitable for small gardens, but only because of the quantity you need to grow. In every other respect, it is an outstanding vegetable and your own will be much better than any shop-bought spinach. It also freezes exceptionally well. When cooked, all three wilt down dramatically, so you need to allow for this when calculating how much to pick.

SUMMER SPINACH

Home-grown summer spinach (*Spinacia oleracea*) has an exquisite buttery taste and creamy texture, equally delicious raw or cooked. Because it wilts down so much on cooking, you need to grow at least three or four rows to give you anything like worthwhile quantities. But it makes an excellent 'catch crop' between peas and brassicas and, if you grow it early, is harvested in good time to follow with other salad crops, French beans, or any crop sown or transplanted from mid-summer onwards. Where space is very restricted, grow the plants close together, harvesting them when small to eat raw in salads. Larger leaves can be blanched and used in various ways – to wrap around fillets of fish, or line vegetable terrines, for example – which look lovely and make maximum use of a small crop.

Cultivation: Summer spinach is best grown in spring, when conditions are cool and moist. It bolts readily in hot weather and is not a good high summer crop. It is fast-growing, can be picked very young, and likes shade. I would also strongly recommend keeping the crop under horticultural fleece until the plants are nearly full grown. This will give you faster and therefore even more tender spinach. A moist, rich, well-drained soil is best. Sow the seeds 1 in (2.5 cm) apart and 1 in (2.5 cm) deep from March to May, spacing rows 9 in (23 cm) apart. Thin progressively to 3–4 in (7.5–10 cm) apart – or 6 in (15 cm) if you want large plants – using the thinnings in salads. It grows 6–9 in (15–23 cm) high, large plants spreading to around 12 in (30 cm), and matures in eight to ten weeks. Two rows minimum; for a sizable crop allow four to six rows.

Recommended varieties: Modern varieties, such as 'Dominant' and 'Norvak', have less oxalic acid, which gives spinach its sharpness. These are excellent, the ones to choose for flavour. Varieties such as the F1 hybrid 'Triton' and 'Cabalero', which are bolt-resistant, are also good.

Harvesting and culinary uses: Start picking when the leaves are 3–4 in (7.5–10 cm) long – large leaves can reach 9 in (23 cm) – going over each plant in turn. Nip the leaf, leaving the stalk on the plant – this saves cutting the stalk off in the kitchen, a useful tip if you have a lot of spinach to prepare. Do not allow the leaves to wilt; either place them in a plastic bag as you pick them or bring inside immediately (see pp. 76–8).

Once it is ready, spinach needs to be picked regularly. You can expect three or four pickings over 10–14 days or so; thereafter the spinach will bolt, producing a central stem and flower spike and sharper-flavoured, angular leaves. These are useful for stuffings and sauces but do not taste as good. Spinach is excellent with roast meat, eggs, cheese, fish and poultry. Small quantities can be used in stuffings, soups and stir-fried.

SWISS CHARD

This tall, strikingly handsome plant (*Beta vulgaris* var. *cicla*) has large crinkly leaves, each with a fat creamy midrib. It is one of the best and easiest to grow of all green leaf vegetables. The leaves have a spinach-like flavour but are more resilient in texture. The midribs are known as chards; these have a mild, neutral flavour and are often cooked separately. Like all dark green vegetables, Swiss chard is high in vitamin C and contains the two essential dietary fatty acids, linoleic and linolenic fatty acids, believed to be protective against heart disease.

Ruby chard is a red-stemmed variety, which can make a very decorative addition to the flower border. It is grown and used in the same way. I find it coarser in flavour, but some gardeners prefer it.

mature and the leaves can reach 2 ft (60 cm) tall. Young plants, taken as thinnings at 9–12 in (23–30 cm) tall, are a delicacy. Plants which survive the winter will resprout in spring. Three or four plants ample.

Recommended varieties: Named varieties perform better than unnamed varieties. 'Fordhook Giant' and an Italian variety, 'Bietola da coste verde AC Argentata', available from Suffolk Herbs (see p. 123), are both excellent.

Harvesting and culinary uses: Pick as required, going over each plant in turn once the plants have become well established, taking the leaves from the base. The leaves are mildest and most tender in early summer, when the plant is growing fast and the weather is cool, or in autumn, again when the weather is cool. For a constant supply, pick regularly. Swiss chard stores extremely well for up to a week: follow directions on pp. 76–8, cutting off the stalks first. Use the leaves in the same ways as spinach. Serve the chards with a creamy sauce or gratinéed, peeling away the stringy outside skin.

Cultivation: Swiss chard is best grown either in spring for early summer use, or in late summer for autumn use. It is a vigorous grower, supplying leaves over a long period of time, tolerant of a wide range of soils and conditions, though a fertile, moist, well-drained soil is best. It bolts readily in hot conditions and does not withstand frosts without protection.

For summer use, sow the seeds in shallow drills 1 in (2.5 cm) apart in April, allowing 12 in (30 cm) between rows. Thin gradually to 12 in (30 cm) apart. For autumn and winter use sow direct in early August, either in a cold frame or using cloches to protect the crop when the weather turns cold. Swiss chard takes about eight to ten weeks to

SPINACH BEET

Spinach beet (*Beta vulgaris*) or perpetual beet, like Swiss chard, is closely related to beetroot. It looks and tastes like coarse spinach and is an extremely hardy, useful winter vegetable which lasts well into spring, when it produces lots of new leaves. Another of my favourite winter vegetables, it's a good choice for small gardens because it provides greens throughout the winter yet is a compact grower.

Cultivation: Sow the seeds 1 in (2.5 cm) apart in shallow drills in August, allowing 9 in (23 cm) between the rows, thinning to 6 in (15 cm) apart. The plants reach about 6–9 in (15–23 cm) tall and take about eight weeks to mature. For larger, more tender leaves, cover with cloches over winter (see pp. 38–9). Two to four rows sufficient.

Recommended varieties: There are no specific varieties of spinach beet. It is sold

as 'spinach beet' or 'perpetual beet' in seed catalogues.

Harvesting and culinary uses: Pick as required, when the leaves are 4–8 in (10–20 cm) long, going over each plant in turn. The flavour varies with the growing conditions: in mild weather it can reach the quality of true spinach, very tender and mild-tasting, as are the young leaves generally. Over winter, it becomes coarser in texture and flavour. Wash thoroughly. I also prefer to remove the midribs – a quick way to deal with these is to turn the leaf over, hold the midrib with one hand and the leaf with the other, and give a sharp tug downwards. Leaves store for a few days in a plastic bag in the fridge. Use as for spinach, in soups and stir-fries.

Roots

Root crops grow successfully in a wide range of soils and conditions, but do best in friable, reasonably fertile soils which have an open structure and free drainage. They tend not to transplant well so are generally sown direct. Ideally, root crops intended for winter supplies should be sown early enough to mature by late autumn, but late enough so that they do not mature too early and become big, tough and woody. As a general guideline, sow at the later times recommended for each variety.

Summer turnips and kohl rabi are included here because they are harvested and eaten as roots. Botanically, they are members of the *Brassica* family, and you should keep this is mind when planning crop rotation (see pp. 36–7).

HARVESTING AND STORING ROOT CROPS

Conventional gardening wisdom says that most root crops may be lifted and stored in boxes of sand or peat, or can be left in the ground and dug when required. My advice generally is to lift root crops in autumn and store them inside. This is more convenient for the cook, and prevents damage to the crops.

Choose a dry day and ease out the vegetables gently with a fork, being very careful not to dig too close to the plant and risk damaging the roots. Clean off the soil and twist off the tops; I also like to leave mine spread out for a few hours to dry off. Arrange in layers in boxes (cardboard boxes are sturdy enough), starting with a layer of sand, peat or coir, or even spent compost. Spread the roots evenly, not touching each other, then cover completely, building up alternate layers as you go. Store somewhere cool. Most roots store well for two to three months, or even longer. Eventually, they begin to dry out and the tops start to sprout (these can be picked and added to salads), but the flavour usually remains good.

BEETROOT

Beetroot (*Beta vulgaris*) is a member of the Goosefoot family *Chenopodiaceae*, so called because many of its species are supposed to have leaves shaped like a goose's foot. It is closely related to spinach beet and Swiss chard. It is high in beta-carotene (see p. 46) and fibre, and has a reputation for being a powerful liver cleanser and blood builder. Summer beetroot is ideal for small gardens. If space permits, I also recommend the autumn-maturing cylindrical beetroot 'Forono', which develops long, beautifully sweet roots, and which you cannot buy. The roots stand proud of the soil and are good value where space is limited. Yellow beetroot ('Burpee's Golden') is becoming more popular and does not bleed.

Cultivation: Summer beetroot is prone to bolting, especially if sown too early; for early crops sow bolt-resistant varieties. It grows well under horticultural fleece. Each knobbly, corky seed consists of a cluster of seeds. Sow from March to end April, when conditions are suitable, spacing each seed 1 in (2.5 cm) apart, allowing 6–8 in (15–20 cm) between the rows, and thin to 2–3 in (5–7.5 cm) apart. Successional sowings can be made until June. Summer beetroot takes about 10–12 weeks to mature and grows to around 9 in (23 cm) tall. One or two rows sufficient.

For mini-beetroot, space summer beetroot about 1 in (2.5 cm) apart and harvest when the size of a ping-pong ball. 'Monaco' is a good variety. One or two rows sufficient.

For autumn beetroot, sow main crop varieties in early June as above, thinning to about 6 in (15 cm) apart. 'Forono' produces thick, cylindrical roots up to 9 in (23 cm) long. One row sufficient.

Recommended varieties: Summer beetroot: 'Boltardy', 'Dwergina', 'Monaco', 'Ramses'. Autumn beetroot: 'Forono', 'Pablo', 'Detroit' cultivars.

Harvesting and culinary uses: Summer beetroot should be pulled while young and tender, about 1–2 in (2.5–5 cm) wide. Pull as required. Harvest autumn beetroot sometime in late autumn *before* the frosts arrive.

> **SOWING TIP**
>
> The corky layer around beetroot seeds contains compounds which can inhibit germination. Soaking the seeds in water for a few hours washes out the natural inhibitors and aids germination

Raw beetroot has a powerful, earthy taste. It needs to be peeled and very finely grated. Mix with orange juice, yoghurt or sour cream, or with finely grated carrot or apple, and serve in small quantities. Cooked beetroot may be grated and tossed in the pan with butter and herbs or spices, or grilled with a savoury breadcrumb topping

CARROTS

Like beetroot, carrots (*Daucus carota*) can be grown either as a summer or autumn-maturing crop. For small gardens, early or summer carrots are ideal. They are smaller, can be deliciously sweet, and are ready to pull in about 12 weeks. My particular favourites are the small round carrots such as 'F1 Rondo'. Carrots are also one of the healthiest vegetables to eat. They are rich in vitamin A, contain other vitamins and minerals including vitamin C, and are one of the most valuable sources of beta-carotene (see p. 46).

Cultivation: Carrots grow best in light, rich sandy soils; never sow on freshly manured ground as this causes the roots to split. With very early varieties, the seeds can be sown direct under cloches or in a cold frame in February, giving early carrots for pulling in May.

Direct sowings of summer carrots can be made from early spring when conditions are suitable. Sow very thinly in shallow drills, 6 in (15 cm) apart. Cover with horticultural fleece; I keep this in place until the carrots are nearly full grown, removing it only if the

CARROT ROOT FLY

This is a persistent pest which must be guarded against. The tiny fly overwinters in the soil, emerging from May to June. It is attracted to the scent of the carrots, laying its eggs nearby in the soil. The small white maggots then burrow into the roots and feed on the carrots; if the damage is severe the carrot will be inedible. After a month, the larvae pupate in the soil to produce a second generation in August and September.

● The chemical treatment for carrot root fly is to use a soil insecticide such as Bromophos granules, but there are several safe remedies which are preferable and will contain the problem so that damage is minimal.

● *Forming a barrier:* Physical barriers can reduce the damage by about 80 per cent. Horticultural fleece is the best and simplest. Make sure it is well secured to the ground during the danger period in late spring and early summer. An open-topped frame 18–30 in (45–75 cm) high put in place immediately after sowing is another effective physical barrier.

● *Sowing time:* By either sowing very early, in March, or sowing very late, at the end of May or in early June, it is possible to avoid the main carrot fly season.

● *Good husbandry:* Disturb the crop as little as possible during the carrot fly season to avoid releasing the scent. Never leave carrot thinnings lying around the vegetable garden.

weather gets hot. Successional sowings can be made until June.

Thinning carrots is the most fiddly job in the garden; you can get away with not thinning them, but I find it preferable, and you will get bigger and more uniformly sized carrots if you do. Thin summer carrots once to 1 in (2.5 cm) apart when the plants are about 2 in (5 cm) high. Carrots grow to around 9 in (23 cm) tall. Water in dry weather. Mini-carrots are grown in the same way, but don't need thinning and are harvested sooner, at finger size. One to two rows minimum; three to four rows ideal.

Recommended varieties: 'F1 Rondo', 'Rocket', 'French Frame', 'F1 Panther', 'Amsterdam Forcing'. Mini-carrots: 'Ideal'.

Harvesting and culinary uses: There is no point in growing a carrot just because it looks pretty, so although summer carrots can be pulled as small as you like, at up to ½ in (1.2 cm) thick, my advice is to wait until the flavour has developed – another two weeks or so can make a noticeable difference. I find a thickness of about 1–1½ in (2.5–4 cm) is generally about right. Pull as required; in heavy soils you may need to use a hand fork, easing it gently by the side of the row. Summer carrots are a real treat, and delicious raw. Cooked, treat them as a gourmet vegetable. They are lovely with mint, tarragon, chervil or basil, or mixed with a creamy garlic purée.

SUMMER TURNIP

Small, tender turnips (*Brassica rapa*) are one of the delights of early summer. The secret is to catch them young – which makes them fine for small gardens. I particularly recommend the mini-turnip, 'Tokyo Cross'.

Cultivation: Summer turnips grow fast and tolerate a wide range of soils, but need moisture to prevent them becoming woody or too peppery in flavour. Early maturing varieties can be sown from mid-February under cover, or direct when conditions allow from March, and successionally until

early June. Sow thinly in shallow drills, spacing the seeds 1 in (2.5 cm) apart, allowing 9–12 in (23–30 cm) between the rows; turnips have a lot of green top and need space. Thin to 2 in (5 cm) apart. Cover spring sowings with horticultural fleece for a faster crop. They take eight to ten weeks to mature and reach about 9 in (23 cm) tall. Watch out for flea beetle attacks (see p. 71). Two to three rows ample.

Sow mini-turnips as above, harvesting approximately eight weeks later, at golf-ball size. No thinning is required.

Recommended varieties: Early maturing: 'Snowball', 'Purple Top Milan'. Mini-turnip: 'Tokyo Cross'.

Harvesting and culinary uses: Pick from when they reach the size of a golf ball, and no larger than a tennis ball. Young turnips have paper-thin skins and do not need peeling. They can be grated raw in salads and are delicious roasted or cooked in a covered pan with butter and a sprinkling of sugar. The very young tops can be used as a green vegetable, in stir-fries.

KOHL RABI

Kohl rabi (*Brassica oleracea* 'Gongyloides') has a strange-sounding name, and even stranger looks, like a pale green or purple sputnik with wavy arms. It is used and thought of as a root vegetable – often described as the turnip-rooted cabbage, though its edible part is the swollen basal part of the plant stem. It has a bland apple-cum-cauliflower flavour, slightly nutty, with a lovely apple crunch when eaten raw. Like

turnip, it may be grown as a summer or autumn-maturing vegetable; for small gardens, it is most useful as a fast-maturing summer crop. I particularly recommend the mini-kohl rabi, 'Rolano'.

Cultivation: Kohl rabi withstands drought, heat and clubroot well, making a reliable alternative to turnips. Sow from March to June in shallow drills, thinning to 3–4 in (7.5–10 cm) apart, allowing 8 in (20 cm) between the rows. For tender bulbs, keep well watered. The plants reach about 12 in (30 cm) tall and mature in eight to twelve weeks. One to two rows sufficient.

Sow mini-kohl rabi as above, spacing the plants 1–2 in (2.5–5 cm) apart, harvesting the bulbs at the size of a golf ball or slightly larger. Pull every other bulb, leaving the remainder to grow on, and pull those as required.

For autumn kohl rabi, sow June to July, thinning to 4–6 in (10–15 cm) if you want larger bulbs.

Recommended varieties: White: 'White Vienna', 'Lanro', 'Rowel F1'. Purple: 'Purple Vienna', 'Delicatess'. Mini-kohl rabi: 'Rolano'.

Harvesting and culinary uses: Kohl rabi is best when the bulbs are small, up to 4 in (10 cm) across; they can become tough and woody when too large. Pull as required, and strip off the leaves. Store as other autumn

roots. It may be peeled and grated or sliced for salads, or cooked in the same way as summer turnip, removing the skin either before or after cooking. Peel, parboil and roast with the joint, or serve in a cream and dill sauce.

HAMBURG PARSLEY

Hamburg parsley (*Petroselinum crispum* var. *tuberosum*) is a variety of parsley, also called turnip-rooted parsley. It is grown for its

delicate parsley-cum-celeriac, sweetish-flavoured tap root and is an excellent vegetable for small gardens, especially if you want to try growing an unusual vegetable which you cannot buy. The leaves are a bonus: they remain green all winter, have a strong parsley flavour and can be used in exactly the same way as ordinary parsley. Hamburg parsley is susceptible to carrot fly (p. 59).

Cultivation: Hamburg parsley tolerates fairly poor soils and some shade, but the seeds are slow to germinate and should not be sown until the soil is warm. Sow direct in shallow drills from early April to May, thinning to 6–9 in (15–23 cm), and allowing 6 in (15 cm) between the rows. It takes around six months to mature and is ready to pull from October to November. The leaves grow to around 9 in (23 cm) tall. The roots are variable in size, 6–8 in (15–20 cm) long and up to 3 in (7.5 cm) wide, but may be smaller. One or two rows sufficient.

Recommended varieties: Hamburg parsley is usually sold just as 'Hamburg' or 'turnip-rooted parsley', though it is better to choose a named variety, such as 'Berliner', if available.

Harvesting and culinary uses: Hamburg parsley is extremely hardy, so can be left in the ground on light soils, or lifted and stored as for other root crops (see p. 57). It is delicious raw, grated finely to use in salads,

makes an excellent soup, or can be cooked and served as other root vegetables.

SUMMER RADISH

I cannot imagine anyone with any sort of garden, however tiny, not growing summer radishes (*Raphanus sativus*). The best radishes – mild and juicy – are grown in spring and early summer. Later on, they become hot and peppery however young you pull them; so much so I do not bother growing them in high summer.

Cultivation: Summer radishes are ready to eat in four to six weeks – pop them in wherever convenient. Once mature they do not last, becoming woody and hot; so sowing little and often is the golden rule. They prefer light soils and cool, moist conditions.

Make the first sowings from February under cover. Sow thinly and evenly, spacing the seeds 1–2 in (2.5–5 cm) apart. Sowings made throughout spring grow well under horticultural fleece. Watch out for flea beetle attacks (see p. 71).

Recommended varieties: 'Durabel', 'Short Top Forcing', 'Cherry Belle', 'French Breakfast', 'Riesenbutter'.

Harvesting and culinary uses: Pull radishes as required and eat fresh. To keep for two to three days, twist off the tops and put immediately into a plastic bag; store in the fridge. Radishes can be revived and re-crisped by soaking in cold water. Use in salads, whole or sliced thinly, and as an appetizer to serve with drinks.

WINTER RADISH

Winter radishes (*Raphanus sativus*) are becoming popular. These are much larger and hardier than summer radishes, both the red- or black-skinned varieties and the milder long, plump, tubular, white-skinned mooli, which rise out of the soil and can easily weigh 2 lb (900 gm) and grow to 12 in (30 cm) long or more. Which to choose is a question of personal taste. I prefer the mooli, but only because in my garden they are consistently mild and succulent. They take around four months to mature, but are excellent value for the space occupied and store exceptionally well.

Cultivation: As for summer radish. Sow in shallow drills from late July to early August, allowing 9 in (23 cm) between the rows, thinning to 4–6 in (10–15 cm) apart. One row ample.

Recommended varieties: 'China Rose', 'Black Spanish Round'. Mooli: 'Mino Early', 'April Cross'.

Harvesting and culinary uses: Winter radishes survive frost, but I find it is much better to bring them inside. Mooli are less hardy, and should be harvested in late autumn; don't be caught out – a bad frost can ruin their taste and texture. Wrapped in a plastic bag, they will keep two to three months in the fridge. The skins of the red and black varieties look attractive when the radish is chopped, but can also be peeled if you wish, using a potato peeler. Use chopped, sliced or grated in salads and stir-fries.

Peas and beans

Peas and beans are one of the most important kitchen garden crops, and there is an enormous range of varieties to choose from. Apart from their culinary and nutritional attractions, they are important nitrogen fixing plants, due to the activity of nitrifying bacteria which live in swellings (nodules) in their roots. The bacteria need a slightly alkaline environment; which is why lime should be always applied if necessary when growing peas or beans, sprinkled over the soil and raked in just prior to sowing or planting. Once the crop is finished, the roots should be left in the ground to decompose and release their store of nitrogen for other crops (see pp. 36–7 for crop rotation). This takes 6–8 weeks in warm weather, longer in cool conditions. The leaves are also particularly high in nitrogen and make excellent compost material.

Peas and beans need not, generally speaking, be watered until they start to flower. Regular watering at the plant base should then be given throughout flower and pod formation; if water is short, give them two good waterings, the first when the flowers start to open, and the second when the pods are swelling.

Peas and beans are among the most rewarding garden crops, but different varieties do seem to perform better than others. Select varieties to suit your conditions, especially if you live in colder parts of the country.

SUGAR SNAP PEAS

Garden peas (*Pisum sativum*) are one of life's great luxuries. The problem is that they aren't really suitable where space for vegetables is at a premium, as the final yield is so small. For small gardens, however, sugar snap peas provide the perfect answer. These have succulent edible, fleshy pods surrounding the peas and the whole pod is eaten (so no waste); they are especially good raw. The fashionable mangetout – another 'eat all' pea – is similarly good value. Both are prolific croppers. The difference between them is that sugar snap pea pods contain fully formed peas, whereas mangetout have thin pods and are eaten before the peas have developed. Of the two I prefer sugar snap peas, finding them sweeter and much juicier. New dwarf varieties such as 'Nofila' (15 in/38 cm) and 'Sugar Rae' (2 ft/60 cm) are ideal size-wise for small gardens, though I generally find the taller varieties have a better flavour. These need to be grown on a wigwam, trellis or fence.

Cultivation: Peas need a fertile, moisture-retentive, slightly alkaline soil, not recently manured (this produces too much leaf at the expense of pods), and prefer a warm, sheltered position. They should *never* be sown in cold, wet conditions or planted out without protection until all danger of frost is past. Early crops (June) should be started off inside. The best method is to use guttering pipe, cut to the length of your row. Fill three-quarters full with compost, sow the seeds thickly in mid-March, water well, and cover with damp peat or coir (see p. 110). This produces a sturdy thicket of young peas to be planted out when 3–4 in (7.5–10 cm) high, under cloches or horticultural fleece when suitable, sometime in late spring.

Don't break them up when planting out; hold a small fork against the peas, pull the piping steadily away from them and slide them out whole into a prepared shallow trench. Alternatively, sow direct fairly thickly in flat, shallow drills, 4 in (10 cm) wide, from early May to mid-June, soaking the seeds first in paraffin to deter mice. Allow about 18 in (45 cm) between the rows. Support with netting propped up with canes or pea twigs when about 6 in (15 cm) high. If birds become a problem, entwine with black cotton. They are ready to eat in 12–15 weeks. One or two rows is sufficient.

Recommended varieties: Dwarf sugar snap: 'Nofila', 'Sugar Rae', 'Sugarbon'. Dwarf mangetout: 'Dwarf Sweet Green'. Tall sugar snap: 'Oregon Sugar Pod'. Tall mangetout: 'Carouby de Maussane'.

Harvesting and culinary uses: Sugar snap peas should be picked when the pods are fully formed, not before; this is when their sweetness has properly developed. Try a few to see. Once ready they last about seven days on the plant – do not leave them to get too old and starchy. (A sure sign is when the pods show brown markings and become misshapen.) Pick regularly to encourage new pods.

Mangetout peas should be picked *before* the peas have formed; this is when they are tender and at their best. They are not as sweet-tasting as sugar snap peas (it's more in the crunch with mangetout) and the pods get tough and misshapen once the peas have formed; they can still be picked and eaten but are not as fine a vegetable.

To prepare both, remove the stringy thread down one side with a quick pull. Chop and add to salads, soups, stir-fries. They need one or two minutes cooking only. Both make excellent summer pea soups.

FRENCH BEANS AND CLIMBING BEANS

French beans (*Phaseolus vulgaris*) are a god-send for small gardens: prolific, cropping well for a long period, decorative enough for the flower border, and they can be harvested when the pods are young or old. Of the dwarf varieties I would choose the pencil-slim haricot verts. The yellow varieties are very attractive and the purple-podded kinds can also be very good, although the colour dulls on cooking. Of the tall climbing beans – to grow up a fence or trellis where space is scarce – my favourite kind is the flat, ribbon type. These have softer skins and a lovely sweet flavour.

Cultivation: Grow in a row as for peas (see opposite). Raise individual plants in 3 in (7.5 cm) pots inside in mid-April, three seeds per pot. Thin to the strongest seedling and transplant out from mid-May under

---

PEA MOTH

Apart from birds, this is the most troublesome pest you are likely to encounter. It lays its eggs in midsummer on flowering pea plants. The caterpillars burrow into the pods, feed off the peas for one month, and then return to the soil to pupate.

● Early (February) or late (May) sowings mean that the peas are not in flower when the pea moth is active. Protect the peas with very fine netting during the flowering season.

● Spray with derris a week after flowering. Dig over the ground in winter on infected plots.

---

cloches or horticultural fleece. Alternatively, sow direct in May or June, 1 in (2.5 cm) deep in a V-shaped drill, spacing the seeds 3 in (7.5 cm) apart. Thin to 6 in (15 cm) apart, allowing 9 in (23 cm) between the rows. Climbing varieties should be grown up a wigwam, or a trellis or netting fixed to the fence.

French beans hate to be cold. Never plant out into cold soil. Cover with horticultural fleece until the plants are well established and the weather has warmed up nicely. Dwarf varieties are bushy, take around 10 weeks to mature and grow to about 12 in (30 cm) tall; climbing varieties take a little

longer and can reach 6 ft (2 metres). One or two rows sufficient. Climbing beans, three to six plants sufficient.

Recommended varieties: Dwarf beans: 'Triomph de Farcy', 'Pros Gitana', 'Royalty', 'Mont d'Or'. Pole beans: 'Blue Lake'.

Harvesting and culinary uses: Pick young dwarf beans 4–6 in (10–15 cm) long, or from about 6 in (15 cm) long for the ribbon type, going over each plant in turn. It is very important to pick French beans regularly – that way new beans will continue to form and give an extended crop. The best way to test for tenderness is to prick the skin with your thumbnail: if it pricks easily, the beans are perfect. Don't worry if the pods are older – French beans make good eating at any time. They remain in good condition in a plastic bag in the fridge for four to five days. Young French beans make lovely salads, blanched for one to two minutes and tossed in sesame seeds or chopped walnuts. Older pods are excellent braised with tomatoes and onions.

Brassicas

The brassicas are a fascinating group of vegetables, but the difficulty with many of them for small gardens is the amount of space they require and the time they take to come to maturity. A Brussels sprout, for example, may be sown in early spring yet not be harvested until late autumn. Squeaky fresh home-grown calabrese is lovely – but excellent calabrese can now be bought virtually all year round. Home-grown cauliflowers are quite exquisite, but are difficult to grow well. Cabbages are easy enough, and can be grown all year, but again can be bought easily – and, at the risk of upsetting traditionalists, who wants cabbage in summer anyway?

So you need to plan which brassicas to grow very carefully and accept that in growing them, even though you can intercrop them with salad stuff while they are young, you have to make sacrifices elsewhere.

The *Brassica* family includes the root crops summer turnip and kohl rabi. Instructions for cultivation are given in the section on Roots, on pages 60 and 61.

GROWING BRASSICAS

Most brassicas require similar growing conditions. To do well, they need a rich, fertile soil, high in organic matter but not recently manured. Where possible, they should follow peas and beans so that they can take advantage of the nitrogen reserves left in the soil. They like a well-drained but firm soil and should be securely staked from an early age. To help deter clubroot (see below), the soil should be alkaline, around pH7, and should be limed if necessary.

For small quantities, raise the plants in small seed trays, thinning the seedlings to 2½–3 in (6–7.5 cm) apart. The ideal size for transplanting is when the plants are 3–4 in (7.5–10 cm) tall (around six weeks old) and have three or four proper leaves – much larger and they do not take as quickly or recover as well, so don't be in a rush to start seeds off too early; the best idea is to calculate your ideal planting out time, and work backwards, sowing four to six weeks earlier. When transplanting, use a trowel, and water the planting hole first. Once the water has soaked away, plant firmly, lightly scratching the top of the soil around the plants so as not to pan the surface. Remove the cotyledons and plant deeply – the stem roots under the ground and helps to anchor the plant firmly against winds.

As a matter of course, keep the brassicas clean, removing dead and dying leaves as they appear. Once mature plants show signs of deterioration, harvest and store inside rather than leave them to deteriorate further.

CABBAGE

Homegrown cabbage can be extraordinarily good, sweet and nutty and not in the least drab or uninteresting. For small gardens, however, you need to be selective. Although you can grow them all year round, my choice would be early autumn-maturing cabbages, such as 'Hispi', and dark green spring cabbages, also known as collards, which remain small all winter but heart up during spring and last well into early summer. Cabbages can grow fearfully large; not a good idea. For small gardens, cabbages bred to produce small heads – such as 'Minicole', which stands well for a couple of months – are often a better choice.

Cultivation: Sow and transplant as described on p. 69. Planting distances vary – closer spacings will result in smaller heads. As a general guideline, allow around 10 in (38 cm) apart.

Cabbages for eating from July to late autumn (summer/autumn cabbages) should be sown in March to April. Cabbages for eating in late autumn and winter (winter cabbages) should be sown April to May. Four to six plants sufficient.

Spring cabbages are loose-hearted cabbages (though most varieties do, in fact, heart up). Sow in early August to mature the following spring, around April, transplanting the young plants from mid-Septem-

'Hispi F1'

CLUBROOT

Clubroot is a pernicious fungus which attacks the roots of all brassicas, causing them to become knobbly and distorted, and to rot. The plants either remain stunted or collapse. Once the land is infected, there is no known cure but preventive measures can, and should, be taken. Should your garden have clubroot, it is simpler not to bother growing brassicas, but use the space for growing other crops. If no brassicas are grown, the land should be clear of clubroot in seven to ten years.

● Never buy in plants but raise your own in new clean compost and clean sterilized (or new) containers. At all costs, avoid bringing clubroot into the garden via muddy boots or seedlings grown in infected land.

● Clubroot thrives on acid soils. Liming the soil (see p. 16) lessens its impact.

● If you do want to grow brassicas where clubroot is present, raise the plants in individual 5 in (12.5 cm) pots, planting out with the rootball intact when the roots have filled the pot. This will circumvent the worst of the clubroot damage.

CABBAGE-ROOT FLY

This also attacks roots of brassica plants. Visible signs are stunted plants and plants that suddenly wilt for no reason. The adult fly overwinters in the soil and lays its eggs around the base of the young plants in spring, again in midsummer, and sometimes in late summer or early autumn. The small white maggots burrow into the roots and eat them.

● A physical barrier is the best protection. Buy or cut 6 in (15 cm) squares of felt or rubber carpet underlay, and make a slit down one side into the middle. Put one square around the base of each stem to prevent the eggs being laid; it must fit snugly, and be weighed down with a stone (birds peck at them and dislodge them). Alternatively, grow brassicas under a protective cover such as horticultural fleece while young. The chemical control is Bromophos granules.

CATERPILLARS

A caterpillar attack sometime over summer is usually inevitable but does not have to be serious. There are three kinds: the yellow and black caterpillars of the large white cabbage butterfly – you can see these as yellow egg clusters on the underside of the leaf; the solitary green caterpillar of the small white cabbage butterfly; and the large plump, light green or brown caterpillars of the cabbage moth. Tell-tale signs are holes in the leaves and pellets of green, slimy digested matter, usually in the crevices.

● The simplest solution for small gardens is the best: go over the plants regularly, squashing any eggs and removing the caterpillars by hand, checking right down between the leaves to extract every one.

● *Bacillus thuringiensis* is a bacterial biological control, available in powder form, specific to caterpillars. It is mixed with water and sprayed onto the plants. Derris or pyrethrum may also be used.

BRASSICA WHITEFLY

Tiny white flies which live on the underside of brassica leaves and leave a sticky 'honey' residue. They are common, though not serious pests, which survive the winter. Pick off the infected leaves; clear away any debris and remove overwintered plants from the plot before the new season's brassicas are sown or planted.

FLEA BEETLES

These small dark shiny jumping beetles attack brassicas and cruciferous plants such as radish, puncturing tiny holes in the leaves of seedlings and young plants. They appear in April or May, and in August. A severe attack can seriously damage crops. Grow plants under a protective covering, and keep seedlings well watered. A simple trap can be made by spreading thick grease on one side of a piece of cardboard. Pass the cardboard along the top of the plants – the beetles jump up and stick to the greased side. They may also be sprayed or dusted with derris.

spring cabbage

ber to early October, 9-12 in (23-30 cm) apart. Apply a dressing of blood, fish and bonemeal or organic fertilizer at the end of winter to encourage growth. Four to six plants sufficient.

Recommended varieties: Summer/ autumn: 'Hispi F1', 'Hawke F1', 'Minicole F1', 'Red Ruby Ball F1'. Winter: 'Aquarius F1', 'January King', 'Wivoy', 'Ormskirk Late'. Spring cabbages: 'Winter Green' (true loose-hearted cabbage), 'Pixie', 'April'.

Harvesting and culinary uses: All cabbages should be picked when they are firm and have a healthy bloom. Cut the plant just below the base - the remaining stalk will resprout. Wrap in a plastic bag and store in the refrigerator. Cabbage is best shredded and lightly cooked, or stir-fried with walnuts or spices. They may also be stuffed or braised.

KALE

Kale is a vastly underrated winter vegetable, highly nutritious, packed with vitamin C, and exactly right for wintery days. It is clean and easy to pick - a great advantage in British winters. In spring, the flowering shoots are also very good to eat, which almost gives you two vegetables for the price of one. There are two forms, flat-leaved kale and the more familiar curly-leaved kale, or borecole, which looks a bit like a dense, frilly mophead. For small gardens, the dwarf varieties (12 in/30 cm tall) are perfect. Look out for the superb-tasting recent introduction 'Showbor'.

Cultivation: Kale is very hardy and less fussy than most brassicas. Sow at any time from April to early June, transplanting to 15 in (38 cm)

apart, or 6 in (15 cm) apart for dwarf varieties, from June to August, as described on p. 69. Keep free of weeds and firmly staked: the plants grow 2–3 ft (60–90 cm) tall. Depending on when you sow, the leaves will be ready to pick from November onwards. A general fertilizer applied in March will encourage production of side shoots.

For mini-kale, sow dwarf varieties between end July and mid-August, nine seeds per 12 in (30 cm) of row. Closely spaced like this, the plants grow to around 12 in (30 cm) tall and are harvested whole (including the stems) from November. Two to four plants sufficient; six to eight plants of dwarf varieties.

Recommended varieties: Dwarf: 'Dwarf Green Curled', 'Darkibor', 'Showbor'.

Harvesting and culinary uses: Pick as required, taking tender leaves, a few from each plant in turn, leaving the outer coarse ones; new leaf shoots will then form. Pick the flowering side shoots at 3–5 in (7.5–12 cm) long. To prepare the leaves, cut away the midrib if this seems coarse. Use like any dark green cabbage. Cook until just tender, and squeeze out excess moisture before serving. The sideshoots should be blanched for one or two minutes until tender; fry with garlic or dress and eat while warm as a salad. Cooked, chopped, kale is also good added to spring soups made with vegetables and pulses.

PURPLE AND WHITE SPROUTING BROCCOLI

Sprouting broccoli is one of my favourite vegetables, wonderfully tender and sweet. Rather than producing one main head it produces lots of small heads, which grow as side shoots, and matures in spring, at precisely the time you need it most. It makes large plants, 2–3 ft (60–90 cm), but they are also prolific and could easily be grown in the flower border. The purple variety is hardier and tends to be more productive.

Cultivation: Sow from end April to early June, transplanting July to August, 15–24 in (38–60 cm) apart as described on p. 69; close spacings produce smaller plants. Keep free of weeds and firmly staked. Two plants sufficient; four ample.

Recommended varieties: 'Purple Sprouting' (early and late); 'White Sprouting Improved'.

Harvesting and culinary uses: Pick as required when the side-shoots are 4–6 in (10–15 cm) long, cutting them near the stem base, taking some from each plant in turn. Regular picking will ensure that more side-shoots form; these will be smaller but equally delicious. To prepare, strip the leaves and rinse briefly in water. The shoots require minimal cooking, one to two minutes. Drain well and serve in a very hot dish. The leaves are tender and also good to eat blanched and chopped, or added to soups.

BROCCOLETTO

This is a very fast-growing, diminutive form of calabrese available from Suffolk Herbs, which grows 6–9 in (15–23 cm) tall, producing one tiny head; it can be useful for small gardens when you have a bit of space to spare though tends to run to seed quickly, and I have had variable results myself.

Cultivation: Sow or broadcast the seed successively from March to late summer in a fertile soil. Thinning is not essential, but plants thinned to 2½–3 in (6–8 cm) produce fatter, more succulent shoots.

Harvesting and culinary uses: Harvest the whole plant when the head forms, at around six weeks old. Steam or cook very briefly for 30–60 seconds, dress and serve as a salad; or use in stir-fries or with pasta.

SEAKALE

I have a special affection for seakale (*Crambe maritima*). It's one of the few native British delicacies, yet is rarely on sale these days – all the more reason to grow it for yourself. It looks rather like an unruly kale plant with grey-green leaves. The edible part is the stem, which is blanched in spring. Freshly picked, it has a mild, faintly nutty flavour. Its curiosity value alone makes it a perfect candidate for an edible herbaceous border. It takes two years to provide your first picking, but thereafter will crop for many years.

Cultivation: Seakale is originally a sea-shore plant, which gives a clue to the kind of conditions it likes best – a sunny position and light, well-drained soil. Since it is perennial, the soil needs to be reasonably fertile, and given a yearly dressing of seaweed meal.

The easiest and best way to grow seakale is from thongs or root cuttings. Plant them square (shoot) end up about 3 in (7.5 cm) deep in March, 12 in (30 cm) apart. Water well in dry weather and take off any flower stems that appear later on in the year. Next spring, apply a dressing of seaweed meal and leave to grow on as before. Once established, it grows to a sizeable plant, reaching up to 2 ft (60 cm) tall. Feed it annually and take off the flower stems every year. It can also be grown from seed. One or two plants sufficient.

Blanching: To be palatable, seakale must be blanched (see p. 93). Special seakale blanching pots can be bought, which are lovely to look at but very expensive, but any large inverted pot, bucket or dustbin which excludes all the light is satisfactory. Cover the plants once they show real signs of growth in January; once you have harvested the plant, remove the blanching pot and let the plant grow on.

Recommended varieties: There are no named varieties of seakale. Thongs are available from A. R. Paske (see p. 123).

Harvesting and culinary uses: Seakale is usually ready to eat sometime in April or May. The blanched stems are like celery but paler in colour and have a tuft of yellow or pinky brown leaves on top. Don't pick them too soon; wait until they are 6–12 in (15–30 cm) high. They are quite brittle, so pick them carefully from the base, taking care not to damage the crown and making sure you leave enough for the plant to build up strength for the following year. The stems can be stored in a plastic bag for a couple of days in the fridge, but are better cut and eaten fresh. Young, fat stalks are crisp and juicy, excellent in salads or cut into batons to nibble with cheese, instead of celery. To cook, lay the stalks in a single layer in a large pan with ½–1 in (1.2–2.5 cm) of water, and cook for five to ten minutes until tender. Serve with melted butter or hollandaise, or to dunk into a soft-boiled egg.

4

SALAD PLANTS

For anyone new to kitchen gardening, especially with a small garden, salad crops offer tremendous value. They take up little room, are attractive to look at, can be fitted into a flower border or any odd corner, and make ideal edging plants, particularly small ground-hugging plants such as land cress, or the fashionable gaily coloured, frilly-edged lettuces.

The variety of salad plants is enormous, so that every garden can have fresh salad material all year round with very little effort. This chapter contains a representative selection of the best. You may want to grow all of them, or just a few – it really doesn't matter. Start with those you particularly like and build up the range gradually.

Winter salad plants deserve a special mention. It is often presumed that you can't grow salad plants in winter, when in fact the reverse is true. By giving the plants some protection, you can make the kind of salad I describe below from the many chicories and other hardy, small green salad plants included in this chapter, which grow best in cool conditions. These winter salad plants have another bonus. Come early spring, all surge into life and make rapid regrowth lasting until the new season's salads come into production.

MAINTAINING CONDITION

The single most important thing when harvesting – and this applies to all leafy vegetables such as spinach and Swiss chard as well as salad plants and lettuces – is never to let the plants or leaves wilt, even for a few minutes, nor to leave them in the sun. Once they have wilted, they do not keep as well – and lose that fresh crispness which makes them taste so good.

● Once cut bring salad plants and leafy vegetables immediately into the kitchen.

Summer lettuce in perfect condition and ready to eat, protected by an Elizabethan-style barn cloche. Frilly salad bowl 'La Lollo' lettuce adds to the visual appeal of a small vegetable bed and provides salad leaves over several weeks.

Give them a quick rinse under the tap and leave in a cool place; or put them into a plastic bowl and cover tightly with cling film; or put straight into a plastic bag as you pick them, and bring inside immediately.

● To store for a few days, discard any damaged leaves, put the rest unwashed into a plastic bag, squeeze out the air and keep in the salad drawer of the fridge; they will keep perfectly for two to four days.

● Whole plants can be kept fresh for one or two days by standing their roots in 1 in (2.5 cm) of water. Keep somewhere cool.

● Whenever possible wash and dry salad leaves when you come to use them. Once prepared, they will keep up to 24 hours if you cover the bowl with cling film and keep in a cool place. Alternatively, put the lid on the salad spinner, after you have spun the leaves to remove the excess moisture.

● Handle salad leaves gently. Soft-leafed plants such as claytonia, lamb's lettuce, spinach and cabbage leaf lettuce should never be left immersed in water.

MAKING SALADS

However many or few salad plants you have in the garden, the secret of using them well is not to pick a bowlful of any one plant, but to pick a few leaves of each in turn, combining them with herbs to produce a harmony of different tastes and textures.

By adopting this method, very small quantities can be used to make an infinite number of interesting salads, which can be bulked out with shop-bought salads as necessary. Lettuce thinnings also make very good salad material. Fresh herbs such as

CULTIVATION TIPS FOR SMALL AND OVERWINTERED SALAD PLANTS

● During hot weather small salad plants become stronger in flavour and more peppery in taste, and run to seed quickly. Spring and late summer to early autumn sowings produce best results.

● For tender, mild leaves, sow small quantities regularly, especially in summer. Cut frequently and use as cut-and-come-again plants. For small quantities, take a few leaves from each plant.

● For larger leaves, better plants and a milder flavour, from autumn protect small salad plants – land cress, claytonia, lamb's lettuce, rocket – with cloches or a simple wooden frame covered with clear plastic sheeting. Unprotected plants are much smaller, and the leaves tougher and stronger tasting.

● All overwintered salad plants make rapid regrowth in spring, providing ample valuable salad stuff before the new season's salads start to come into production.

mint, chervil, chives, tarragon and dill add a lovely piquancy. Edible flowers make any salad look as pretty as a picture. The golden rule is just to use what is at hand, and what you fancy.

This varied mixture is known as a misticanza salad, or what the Elizabethans called 'saladings'. A few leaves, arranged on individual plates – no need to be fussy – forms the basis of an instant 'designer' salad. To finish, top with tasty ingredients such as strips of red pepper, olives, chopped hard-boiled egg, crispy bacon, tiny cubes of cheese, toasted nuts, croutons, and so on. Add your favourite dressing at the last moment and the salad is ready to eat.

LETTUCE

Lettuces (*Lactuca sativa*) are best grown successionally, choosing varieties to suit the time of year. For small gardens, I would definitely choose early summer lettuces such as 'Tom Thumb', 'Little Gem', 'Fortune', the variegated variety 'Marvel of Four Seasons', and the loose-hearted 'Salad Bowl' lettuce. All can be grown in a border, last well and are very decorative.

There are three main types of lettuce:

Cabbage head: These are flat or round-headed, hearted lettuce. There are two broad types: the soft-leaved, buttery spring, autumn and winter 'butterheads', such as 'Fortune', 'Kwiek' and 'Avon Defiance'; and

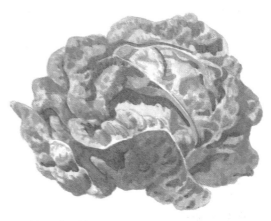

cabbage head lettuce

thick, crisp-leaved summer 'crispheads', such as 'Webb's Wonderful', 'Lakeland' and 'Iceberg', which form bullet-tight hearts and last well.

Cos: These are upright, generally large lettuces, well flavoured, with a distinctive taste and lovely crisp midribs. Both green and red-leaved varieties are available. 'Cosmic' is a first class green variety. 'Winter Density' and 'Little Gem' are excellent small cos types.

Salad bowl lettuces: These lettuces do not form a compact heart but grow as a loose rosette spreading outwards from the centre; they are valuable cut-and-come-again plants. There are two main varieties, the frilly-edged 'Lollo Rossa' (the red version is particularly attractive) and the indented-leaved, green and red 'Salad Bowl'. I also highly recommend the Italian oak-leaved varieties available from Suffolk Herbs. Their flavour and texture is slightly coarser than other varieties of lettuce, and for this reason they are best used a few leaves at a time to add colour and variety to other lettuces and salad plants.

cos lettuce

Cultivation: Lettuces grow best in fertile soil. They like plenty of moisture and bolt in hot conditions. Sow small quantities frequently, every three weeks in shallow drills. Start thinning as soon as the plants have two true leaves, at about ½ in (1.2 cm) tall, to 1 in (2.5 cm) apart, gradually thinning to their final spacing, using the thinnings in salads. The final spacing depends on size of mature plant: 5–6 in (13–15 cm) for small varieties;

9 in (23 cm) for cabbage head; 12 in (30 cm) for large cos and crispheads.

Lettuces can be raised very successfully in small pots, which give the most flexibility. Transplant carefully when four proper leaves have formed, at about 1 in (2.5 cm) high. They may also be grown as a seedling crop, by broadcasting a small patch of seeds and cutting the young leaves when 3–4 in (7.5–10 cm) high – salad bowl types are best. Pick off any rotting leaves to help prevent mildew. Depending on the variety and

Aphids

Lettuces are susceptible to aphid attack, particularly poorly grown specimens. Pick off by hand or spray with derris.

Root aphid

This causes lettuce to keel over in August and September for no apparent reason, and shows as little white grubs in the root. Rotate lettuce and grow resistant varieties such as 'Avon Defiance' and 'Beatrice' for sowings made after mid-summer.

Slugs

Seedlings and young plants need protection from slugs, such as a plastic bottle mini-cloche (see p. 39).

Mildew

A problem in damp weather. Remove and burn infected leaves and plants, avoid condensation (keep cloches and coverings well ventilated), and grow resistant varieties such as 'Sigmahead' and 'Beatrice'.

salad bowl lettuce

time of year, lettuces take between 10 and 14 weeks to mature. Six plants of headed varieties, and two to three plants of loose-leaved varieties sufficient for each batch grown.

Harvesting and culinary uses: Lettuces reach perfection on maturity, not before. Look for the bloom and check that the heart is firm. Generally speaking, they remain at

WHEN TO SOW LETTUCES

Lettuce seed germinates well at low temperatures; conversely, lettuce does not germinate well at high temperatures and in summer germination can be poor and erratic. Choose butterhead and salad bowl varieties for spring and early summer and crisphead and cos varieties for main summer sowings. For later sowings, root aphid resistance is important. In hot conditions, water the drill well, and keep the seedbed moist until germination occurs.

SUCCESSIONAL SOWING CHART FOR LETTUCE EARLY SUMMER TO AUTUMN

Variety	When to sow	When to eat
'Tom Thumb' 'Little Gem'	February/March	early summer
'Marvel of Four Seasons' 'Fortune'	March/April	early summer
'Cosmic' (cos) 'Lakeland' (crisphead)	April/early June	summer
'Lollo Rossa' 'Salad Bowl'	March/early June	early summer/summer
'Avon Defiance'	June/mid-August	autumn
'Rouge d'Hiver' 'Marvel of Four Seasons' 'Bruna di Germania' 'Kwiek'	mid-August/ September	late autumn/ early winter

their peak for about a week, though some varieties stand better than others. In wet or dry weather, pick and store inside before lettuce has a chance to rot or bolt. Cut the plant with some stalk attached, and store as described on pp. 76 and 78, to last seven to ten days in the fridge. Loose-leaved lettuces are better picked when the leaves are young or have grown quickly (old leaves are coarse). Pick individual leaves or cut 1 in (2.5 cm) above the base, leaving the plant to resprout. Home-grown lettuces are delicious eaten on their own and excellent with barbecued meat or fish. Lettuce can also be cooked – but don't use old and bolted lettuces which can be coarse-flavoured.

LAMB'S LETTUCE

Lamb's lettuce (*Valerianella locusta*), or corn salad, is a true springtime delicacy. The soft, floppy, tongue-shaped leaves form a ground-hugging rosette about 6 in (15 cm) high and have a lovely mild, gentle flavour. Several varieties exist, some with larger leaves. Together with claytonia (see opposite), it is one of the best plants for winter salads.

Cultivation: Lamb's lettuce is tolerant of most soils and situations. It is extremely hardy and survives frosts well. It grows best in cool conditions, in spring and early autumn. Sow thinly in rows 6 in (15 cm) apart in March, under cover, for an early

summer crop, or in August to early September for an autumn or winter crop. The plants are usually thinned to around 3 in (8 cm) apart; this produces larger plants, but is not absolutely necessary. Young plants can also be transplanted. The plants grow slowly at first, and take up to three months to mature. Once mature, they reach around 6 in (15 cm) across and produce a constant supply of tender, new leaves. One or two rows sufficient.

Harvesting and culinary uses: Start to pick once the plants are well established and the leaves are 2–3 in (5–7.5 cm) long. You can either harvest whole plants, which are particularly attractive in the salad bowl, or single leaves. Cut with a knife just above the base, when the plant will resprout. When washing pay particular attention to the underside of the leaf, which is often dirty from close contact with soil. Use the leaves whole, generously on their own or in any mixed green salad.

ROCKET

Rocket (*Eruca sativa*) looks rather like a young brassica plant, with its wavy-edged leaves, and has a unique peppery, spicy flavour. I find it one of the most versatile salad plants, and it is a must if you like Italian food!

Cultivation: Rocket is a hardy annual that can be grown in any soil or situation, though a moist, fertile soil will produce larger, milder leaves. Spring and early autumn sowings produce the best rocket, succulent and not too peppery. It can be grown throughout summer, but needs a shady position. Plants which survive the winter resprout in spring.

Sow thinly from early March in shallow, broad drills, making the first sowings under cover. No thinning is required. The leaves are ready to pick in approximately six to eight weeks. It is difficult to say how much rocket you may need. Aficionados (like myself) love it and can eat it by the handful, but others find it overpowering and need very little. If you use a lot, the best idea is to sow successionally. Otherwise, a half to one row should be sufficient.

Harvesting and culinary uses: Rocket is best when the leaves are young and the plants 4–6 in (10–15 cm) high; or when it has been grown very fast under cover, which produces much larger but also mild-tasting leaves. Cut with a knife or scissors as required, 1 in (2.5 cm) or so above the ground, leaving the plants to resprout. It is excellent with tomatoes, Italian cheeses and potato, bean and pasta salads. Chopped leaves add a tangy zest to green salads, omelettes and pasta stuffings.

CLAYTONIA

Claytonia (*Claytonia perfoliata*), also called miner's lettuce or winter purslane, is one of the best and prettiest of all winter salad plants. It is perfect for small gardens: prolific, compact, easy to grow, delicious to eat, and able to survive any frost. The dainty lime green leaves form bushy whorls like a ballerina's skirt and produce edible white, starry flower spikes as spring progresses. The mild leaves are rich in vitamin C and have a succulent, slightly fleshy texture.

Cultivation: Claytonia will grow anywhere, though a damp and shady position is preferable. Broadcast a small patch of seed in August for autumn and winter use. The plants soon form a dense carpet and may be transplanted out into clumps about 6 in (15 cm) apart (dig up with a good ball of soil) if too dense. The plants reach 6 in (15 cm) high and will be ready to pick in four to six weeks. A patch of 2–3 sq ft (60–90 sq cm) sufficient.

Harvesting and culinary uses: Use as a cut-and-come-again plant, snipping off the leaves by the handful; new leaves resprout quickly. They bruise easily, so wash very

briefly. It can be used generously with any green salad. It combines well with beetroot and can also be cooked and used in soups – for example, with leeks and peas.

LAND CRESS

Land cress (*Barbarea verna*), also known as American, Belle Isle or winter cress, is another invaluable salad plant for small gardens, especially in winter. It looks and tastes very similar to cultivated watercress (*Nasturtium officinale*), but is slightly stronger in flavour and has smaller, slightly tougher leaves. It grows as a flat rosette about 6 in (15 cm) high, the leaves spreading out from the centre like the points of a compass, and makes a good edging plant.

Cultivation: Land cress is extremely hardy, keeping its dark green leaves throughout winter. It does well in damp, shady places and north-facing spots, so is useful for odd corners or intercropping between tall plants such as brassicas. It likes a moist, rich soil: hot, dry soils should be avoided. The best time to sow is August to early September for autumn and winter use, and into the following spring; I also sow it in April for early summer use. Sow in shallow drills. It may be thinned to 3 in (7.5 cm) apart, though this is not strictly essential as, like lamb's lettuce, it grows happily without. It may also be transplanted, and takes eight to ten weeks to mature. Six well-grown plants (half a row)

icate, lacy-looking, finely divided leaves, similar to those of flat-leaved parsley, which have a biting, peppery taste becoming very hot as they mature.

Cultivation: Garden cress, a hardy annual, is one of the easiest plants to grow. It prefers light, moist soils, but can be grown anywhere outside or in a tray on the windowsill. The young seedlings quickly produce a

should be sufficient; more if you want to use it instead of watercress for making soup.

Harvesting and culinary uses: Begin to harvest once the plants are sufficiently large and established. The leaves can be taken at any size; I usually choose the inner, tender leaves when they are 2–4 in (5–10 cm) long. Pick a few from each plant as required, or cut with scissors 1 in (2.5 cm) above the ground, leaving the plant to resprout. The leaves store well and will need careful washing – soak in water first to dislodge dirt from the underside of the leaf. Use as watercress – chopped in rice, grain or pasta salads, to flavour sandwich fillings, stuffings, sauces and mayonnaise, to add to stir-fries and to clear soups. Use as a substitute for cultivated watercress to make soups and sauces.

GARDEN CRESS

Garden cress (*Lepidium sativum*) is a member of the *Cruciferae* family and has very del-

thick green carpet and will be ready to eat in about three to four weeks. It grows best in spring or autumn when conditions are cool. Unless you particularly like it, it's not worth growing in summer. Broadcast a small patch, or sow in shallow drills 4–6 in (10–15 cm) wide, from early spring onwards. A patch of 18 sq in (45 sq cm), or one short row (18 in/ 45 cm) ample.

Harvesting and culinary uses: Garden cress is ready to eat as soon as the leaves are 2 in (5 cm) tall, and should be used while they are young. Cut frequently by the handful as a cut-and-come-again plant. The leaves are fiddly to wash – being small and lacy, they tend to stick together. Add to all kinds of salads, or as garnish for clear soups. It imparts a peppery flavour.

Chicories

Chicories (*Cichorium intybus*) are a large group of deep-rooted perennials and very hardy autumn and winter salad plants. Most have a distinctive, more or less bitter flavour, which is why the best way to use them is in small quantities, mixing them with other softer-flavoured leaves. All are trouble free and easy to grow and just a few plants of each type add colour and variety to winter salads, and last right through spring.

To make them milder and more tender, some types of chicories may be blanched or forced. Blanching literally means 'to bleach or make white' and involves putting a top of some kind over the chicory to exclude the light; the leaves become paler and much of the bitterness disappears. This is covered under the entry for endives (see p. 93), which are treated in exactly the same way. Red and green varieties of chicory may be blanched – though whether to do so is very much personal taste. These days, I rarely

bother and enjoy these chicories just as they are.

Witloof chicory must be forced. Forcing involves digging up the roots, cutting off the tops and 'forcing' new blanched shoots to grow by leaving them in total darkness, somewhere warm. The shoots are known as 'chicons' and are the familiar white, crisp, conical chicory found in the shops. Forcing is a simple process and I really do recommend it. Ball-headed and spear-headed chicories can be treated in the same way – though success with these for the home gardener is variable.

RED AND GREEN CHICORIES

There are many varieties of these. The leaves may be red, green, pink, magenta or variegated in colour, intensifiying in winter; and pointed, round or wavy-edged in shape. Some varieties form a loose rosette, some form a tight spear head like a chicon, and others, like radicchio, form a tightly headed ball. Others, like 'Biondissima di Trieste', can be used when the leaves are 2 in (5 cm) high as cut-and-come-again plants. The only one I do not care for is 'Grumolo Verde', which I find tough and uninteresting – though some gardeners think it one of the best. Chicory leaves are tougher than most salad plants and all have a relatively strong flavour, though some varieties are milder. Suffolk Herbs offer the widest selection – and it really is a question of seeing which variety works for you. If you want to grow radicchio, which can also be forced like witloof chicory, choose the new improved varieties such as 'F1 Medusa' or 'Cesare', which form tight heads more easily.

Cultivation: Red and green chicories are very hardy and grow easily in most soils and situations, but are always better if grown under cover. This produces larger, more tender and more reliable plants. Sow direct in shallow drills from June to August, allowing 6–9 in (15–23 cm) between the rows, thinning first to 6 in (15 cm), then to 9 in (23 cm) apart. Alternatively, they can be sown in small pots and transplanted out when 2–3 in (5–7.5 cm) high. Water in dry conditions and keep the plants free of dead or rotting leaves. Depending on the variety, they grow to around 6–9 in (15–23 cm) tall.

As autumn approaches, the ball and spear-headed varieties start to form their tight heads – these are the leaves you use. Some varieties form better heads than others, and it does seem to be a hit and miss affair, so you may need to experiment to see which variety and sowing times work for you. Removing the outside leaves from the ball or spear-headed varieties in early autumn is said to encourage tight heads to form. This is usually the case, but not invariably so. Six to nine plants ample.

Recommended varieties: Red ball type: 'F1 Medusa', 'Rossa di Verona', 'Cesare'. Red spear head: 'Rossa di Treviso' (green foliage in summer, turns red from September). Variegated: 'Variegata di Castelfranco', 'Variegata di Chioggia'. Green, rosette: 'Grumolo Verde'. Cut-and-come-again: 'Biondissima di Trieste'.

Harvesting and culinary uses: Pick the leaves any time from September, when the

plants are mature (you can pick the rosette forms earlier, but there is little point as there are other summer plants to choose from). I pick a few leaves from each plant, all except the outermost coarse leaves; this way, the plants can be harvested right through winter. I do this with those that form tight heads also, but if you want to harvest the whole plant, or the plant shows signs of damage, cut it above the crown and in due course it will resprout.

Because the leaves are tougher than most salad plants, they store very well in a plastic bag in the fridge (see also general storage notes on p. 78). Apart from use in salads, they may be cooked in many delicious ways – painted with olive oil and grilled or barbecued, added to risottos, or baked with Italian cheeses. Small inner leaves are generally milder in flavour. The larger leaves should be torn.

LATE WINTER SALADS

Never write off late-planted winter chicories or endives, however small or unpromising they seem. They grow very slowly or not at all over winter; but once the days begin to lengthen and temperatures start to rise, the plants quickly put on new growth, providing new salad material from late winter until late spring, or whenever they start to bolt. The same applies to hardy lettuces grown under cover.

SUGAR LOAF CHICORY

Sugar loaf chicory is a large, conical-headed autumn chicory, similar to a Chinese cabbage in appearance, solid as a rugby ball because of its densely packed leaves. If you have never grown chicories before, this is the one I recommend you start with. It is a self-blanching chicory, which is to say the leaves wrap themselves around each other so tightly that they blanch themselves, resulting in naturally mild, pale chicory.

Cultivation: Sugar loaf chicory will grow in a variety of soils but to produce desirable large, succulent heads, it needs a fertile, moisture-retentive soil. It is inclined to bolt if sown too early, so wait until June or July. Sow the seeds in a shallow drill, 1 in (2.5

cm) apart, thinning progressively to 9–12 in (23–30 cm) apart. The plants mature in autumn and grow to around 12 in (30 cm) tall. Although they will stand a few degrees of frost, protect the plants from autumn onwards with cloches, which keeps them in better condition. Four to six plants ample.

Recommended varieties: The new improved F1 hybrids, such as 'Jupiter', produce the tightest self-blanched heads. 'Crystal Head' is another good variety.

Harvesting and culinary uses: Harvest as required from October to December. In bad weather, if you cannot protect the plants, harvest them all. They store superbly well for two to three months in a plastic bag in the fridge, one large sugar loaf chicory providing salad material over several weeks. Cut the plants at soil level and remove the outer leaves or any that are damaged. Sugar loaf chicory is best used in salads. Remove the leaves singly, starting from the outside, and shred or tear. Small leaves can be used whole and are good with walnut oil dressings and with chopped boiled egg sprinkled with fried breadcrumbs.

WITLOOF CHICORY

This is a truly delicious salad plant and, contrary to popular opinion, so long as you choose the right varieties, nothing is easier to grow. The old varieties were difficult to force successfully as they tended to form loose chicons. New F1 hybrids such as 'Normato' or 'Zoom' (which really does live up to its name) produce perfect tight forced heads of chicory effortlessly – crisper, fresher, sweeter, and much cheaper than those you buy.

Cultivation: Sow outside in shallow drills, as early as possible when conditions allow in April, thinning to 9 in (23 cm) apart and allowing 9 in (23 cm) between the rows.

FORCING

1 Cut off all the foliage ¼–½ in (6–12 mm) above the crown. Fill large pot(s) two-thirds full with moist (not too damp) spent compost, peat or sand. Trim off all the whiskery side shoots, and trim the roots to fit.

2 Insert the roots, back filling with compost etc, up to their necks. Leave the crown clear, and remember to leave enough space between them to get your fingers in to pick the chicons.

3 Invert a same-sized pot on top, cover the drainage hole to exclude the light, and put somewhere dark; an understairs cupboard is ideal, or somewhere similar with an even temperature of around 50–60°F (10–15°C).

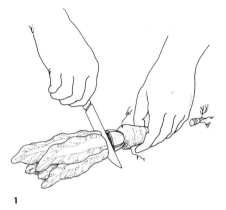

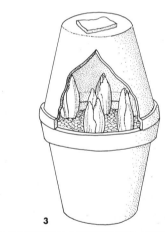

1

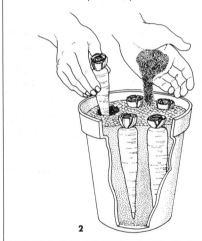

2

3

The plants produce a mass of spear-like green leaves and grow to around 12 in (30 cm) tall. Dig up the roots in late October to November, discarding very small ones.

The roots are now ready to force. Traditionally, roots were stored in sand or peat until required, but I find you get better results if the roots are potted up soon after harvesting, and treated as described below. Twelve plants sufficient for two large forcing pots.

Slow, steady forcing produces the sweetest and best-flavoured chicons with no hint of bitterness, whereas too warm a place induces bolting. Depending on the temperature, the chicons are ready to eat after three to four weeks and remain in good condition for up to eight weeks, or even longer.

To keep the chicons in good condition, it is very important to keep them clean, removing any rotting bits of foliage and to pick them as described below. If aphids appear on the leaves, as they do occasionally, wipe them off with damp paper. Keep the chicons in total darkness at all times – exposure to light rapidly induces greening and the flavour becomes more bitter. If the pot becomes very dry, stand it in a tray of water until the compost is just moist, then allow to drain.

Harvesting and culinary uses: Heads can be cut whole, but unless a whole head is specifically required, a much better method is to pick outside leaves from each plant in turn. This way picking can be extended to several weeks, and the chicons will remain in good condition. When you get to the inner central portion, cut this above the crown – this produces smaller but useful resprouts.

For an instant 'designer' salad, fan the leaves like a star around the plate. Fill the centre with whatever salad you like – pasta, rice, potato, grated vegetables, apple and walnut – sprinkle with herbs and serve. The chicons also make an excellent cooked vegetable.

ENDIVE

Endives (*Cichorium endivia*) look rather like unkempt lettuces with jagged-edged leaves. They are closely related to chicory and have the same bitter flavour, but are not as hardy. Like chicory, they are easy to grow, suffer no pests or diseases, and keep extremely well once cut. There are two types: the hardier broad-leaved batavian endive, and the beautiful frilly frisée endive. I like them both, but would probably choose the frisée kind, which is milder and prettier, if I had never grown endive before.

The leaves of endive are often too bitter to be eaten as they are and so are generally blanched first, by putting a top over the mature plants or tying them up with twine. When light is excluded the leaves become milder, more tender and sweeter in taste, and also much paler in colour, resulting in fresh white and yellow hearts. Growing conditions affect how mild or bitter they

batavian endive

may be and, as with chicories, once you develop a liking for endive's sharp taste, blanching becomes less necessary.

They are usually grown as an autumn and early winter crop, but try them also in summer; they may readily bolt but have a lovely mild flavour. Those that grow sufficiently large are easier to blanch.

Batavian endive, also known as scarole, is most suitable for autumn and winter use, and for overwintering under cover. The plants tend to be larger than those of frisée endive, which is less hardy but better suited to growing in summer as it is more tolerant of heat. It is best in autumn and early winter. It is not as suitable for overwintering as batavian endive (though this is not impossible), and the leaves rot easily in cold, damp weather.

Recommended varieties: Batavian: 'Batavian Green', 'Cornet de Bordeaux', 'Scarole Verde'. Frisée: 'Sally', 'Wallonne' (both tight self-blanching hearts), 'Moss-curled', 'Pancalieri'.

Cultivation: Endives are grown in the same way as lettuce. They prefer a rich, moisture-retentive soil, and, like chicories, succeed best when they are protected by cloches later on. For autumn and early winter use, sow the seed in shallow drills from June to August, watering the seed drill well first, thinning to 6 in (15 cm), then 12 in (30 cm) apart, allowing 9 in (23 cm) between rows. Avoid sowing in hot conditions, as germination is slow and the plants eventually bolt. If this is unavoidable, germinate the seeds somewhere cool and shaded in small pots, transplanting the young plants complete with root ball when 2–3 in (5–7.5 cm) high; this helps to avoid the shock of transplanting which also causes endives to bolt. From early autumn, or if the weather is unseasonally bad, protect with cloches. They are large, slow-growing plants, taking about three months to mature, reaching 9–12 in (23–30 cm) in height and spread. Four to six plants sufficient.

For summer, use frisée endive, sowing direct under cover in March or April when

frisée endive

conditions allow; a shady spot is best. Remove the cover when the plants are established.

Spring sowings do not produce as large plants, as they bolt sooner in response to the lengthening days of summer – but they are just as good to eat.

Blanching: This is carried out when the plants are fully grown and ready to eat. It's easy enough but success is variable, especially for the amateur gardener. The simplest way is to tie the whole plant up tightly like a stuffed cabbage, using twine, wrapping the outside leaves around and over the plant and trussing it up as best you can. You can also put a large upturned pot over the whole plant (cover up the drainage hole). This excludes more light and produces better blanched plants, but they are more likely to

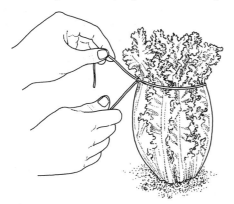

Tie frilly endives firmly with garden twine as shown. In two to three weeks the hearts will be blanched white with attractive pale-lemon-edged leaves which are mild and crisp and ready to eat.

rot. Plastic blanching caps are now available, but I don't find them very satisfactory.

It is imperative to keep the plants dry and free from slugs. Try to ensure that the plants are dry before you begin to blanch them and remove any rotting leaves first. Blanch a couple of plants at a time; they will be ready in two to three weeks.

Summer endives which are large enough to blanch, do so readily without rotting. Tie them with twine as above. They are ready in 10–14 days.

Harvesting and culinary uses: Unblanched endives may be cut whole or picked a few leaves at a time as required, choosing the young leaves. Cut the plants 1 in (2.5 cm) above the ground and leave to resprout. Watch out for bolting, particularly in summer, as the plants become more bitter. Pick and store inside (see pp. 76 and 78) before this occurs. The flavour also becomes more bitter when the weather is hot.

Blanched endives are cut whole and, except in summer, need ruthless trimming, as much of the outside may be rotten. Trim away all but usable heart. If possible, do not wash the plant if you intend to store it. If this is unavoidable (often the case) wash briefly, spin dry, then store in the usual way. An endive should keep for two or three weeks, or even longer. Check from time to time, removing any deteriorating leaves.

Endives are used in the same way as chicory. They may also be braised or grilled.

5

HERBS

Herbs add beauty and fragrance to any garden, attracting bees and other friendly insects from miles around. For small gardens they represent excellent value.

CHOOSING AND GROWING HERBS

Deciding which herbs to grow is a matter of personal preference, but where space is restricted it is worth bearing in mind a few guidelines. For culinary purposes, start with those you like and are likely to find most useful, spreading the range to give some fresh herbs throughout the year. Most are easy to grow and can be fitted in wherever space allows. Few have special requirements and the majority grow very well in containers or in pots kept on the windowsill. Perennial herbs fit easily into flower borders and rockeries, and brighten up odd corners. Avoid large or rampant herbs such as angelica, lovage or fennel, but you may wish to include the occasional herb with edible flowers such as lavender or borage.

You will find that large quantities of herbs are rarely necessary. As a rule of thumb, raise from seed the annuals you find you use most. One packet of seed usually lasts a couple of seasons. Otherwise, it is simpler to buy in a box of young plants for planting out. Perennial herbs can be bought singly, then you can propagate by cuttings to increase stock or grow a new season's plants.

HARVESTING

Although evergreen perennial herbs – rosemary, sage, thyme – can be picked at any time, all herbs are best through spring and summer up to when they flower: the leaves are young and tender, growth is rapid and, as summer progresses, the aromatic oils reach their highest concentration. In hot condi-

A perfect arrangement for a small garden. A selection of kitchen and other herbs grown in a cartwheel add fragrance and beauty all year round. Culinary herbs include marjoram and lemon thyme. A strawberry pot, which can be used to grow herbs, adds extra visual charm and can be placed in any suitable spot on the patio or near the kitchen.

tions, annual herbs run to seed. As autumn approaches, they become stronger, less sweet and tougher.

Pick herbs gently, taking care not to bruise the leaves. This is not so important for tough-leaved plants such as rosemary, but is very important for any herb which has a delicate leaf, such as chervil.

STORING

Most fresh herbs store well for a few days, wrapped either in cling film or in damp kitchen paper, and kept in a plastic box in the fridge.

These days it is no longer necessary to dry culinary herbs unless you especially want to. Freezing them retains their flavour and is more convenient. Only some annual summer herbs are worth freezing: tarragon, parsley and dill freeze best; once thawed, they become soggy but are fine to use in cooking.

FRESH DRIED HERBS

This is an excellent method for preserving small quantities of herbs which you intend using fairly quickly. It works particularly well for oregano, parsley, tarragon and mint. Strip off the leaves, chop finely and leave spread out on a board or work surface to dry for a couple of hours. Use as required. Wrap any surplus in cling film, and they will easily keep in a dark cupboard or in the fridge for a few weeks.

CHIVES

Chives (*Allium schoenoprasum*) are perennial and the bright green cylindrical blades are a most welcome sight in late winter and early spring. They make ideal edging plants, though for culinary purposes a small clump suffices. They have an onion flavour. The pretty purple flowers have the same taste and can be scattered over salads.

Cultivation: Chives need a fertile soil, high in humus – yellowing tops are a sign of nutrient deficiency – and prefer moist conditions. Buy a clump of bulblets in spring and plant 9 in (23 cm) apart. The clumps reach 6–16 inch (15–40 cm) tall and will need dividing to prevent overcrowding, either in spring or autumn. They should be given an occasional feed of nitrogen fertilizer such as dried blood; spent coffee grounds are often recommended for the same purpose, and do work.

Harvesting and culinary uses: Chives are most valuable in spring and early summer, when the stalks are tender; as summer progresses the stalks become increasingly coarse. Snip frequently with scissors 1 in (2.5 cm) or so from the base to encourage new growth. The very young blades, 2 in (5 cm) high, are especially tender.

Chives can be used liberally in salads, soups and simple cream sauces. They are excellent with fish, eggs, soft cheeses, dips, sandwich fillings, cucumber and potatoes. If you have a surplus, whole chive stems can be added to stir-fries, cooked for a few seconds only.

CHERVIL

Chervil (*Anthriscus cerefolium*) has lacy, lime green leaves and is one of the best herbs for spring and early summer. It has a mild, slightly sweetish aniseed taste, akin to that of tarragon. Its delicate foliage and tiny white flowers make it one of the prettiest herbs for edging a border. Valued as a blood cleanser for many centuries, the leaves contain vitamin C, carotene, iron and magnesium.

Cultivation: Chervil is a hardy annual and is best sown in spring, during March or April when conditions are cool, in a shady position and moist but not waterlogged soil.

Alternatively, raise a few plants inside in small individual pots, or buy them ready to plant from a garden centre, planting out at 6–9 in (15–23 cm) apart. It reaches a height of 8–12 in (20–30 cm) (although the flower stalks may grow taller). Transplanted plants run to seed more quickly. Three to six plants ample.

In hot conditions chervil rapidly runs to seed and the leaves become redder and tougher. For a constant supply of new leaves, cut out most of the flower stalks as they appear. Leave some, as chervil readily seeds itself and germinates quickly, so further sowings are rarely necessary. Although chervil is very hardy, the leaves usually die back in winter. Protecting the plant with cloches will help ensure a few fresh leaves and encourage quicker new growth.

Harvesting and culinary uses: Start picking once the plant is established (about 4 in/10 cm high) and use while the leaves are young, preferably before the flower stalks form. Once picked, the leaves wilt immediately and do not store well, so try to pick at the last moment. If wrapped immediately, they will keep for two or three days in the fridge (see p. 96). Chervil makes a lovely aromatic addition to spring and early summer green salads. To retain its delicacy, chervil is never cooked, but added at the end of making sauces and soups. Use with eggs, pancakes, chicken, fish, carrots, potatoes, dips and mayonnaise.

MINT

One of the commonest and most-loved perennial herbs, and one of the first to show through in spring, mint (*Mentha* species) is deliciously refreshing. Few herbs have better medicinal, digestive and soothing properties. It is also one of the few herbs which can be used successfully for both savoury and sweet dishes. Herb centres sell several varieties, ranging from the charming diminutive Corsican mint, which grows

barely more than 1 in (2.5 cm) high, to the common peppermint which reaches 3 ft (1 m) high. Taste before you buy, as the flavour of the different mints varies considerably. For culinary purposes, I still find common spearmint and the hairy-leaved apple mint two of the best.

Cultivation: Mint is generally grown from long portions of root known as 'runners'. Plant them horizontally 2 in (5 cm) deep, in spring after danger of frost has passed, in a rich soil. Ideally, plant in a warm, damp position, sun or light shade, and away from other herbs if possible. Mints are greedy feeders and need an occasional top-dressing of compost or organic fertilizer. They are invasive, and need checking in some way. The usual method is to grow them in a sunken container or even a large plastic bag; make sure there are drainage holes. Slugs love the early spring shoots, which should be protected. A few runners potted up in the greenhouse, or brought inside in autumn, provide some fresh mint during winter. One or two plants sufficient.

Harvesting and culinary uses: Mint can be harvested as soon as the shoots are about 3 in (7.5 cm) high; nip out the top one and the side-shoots will grow. The leaves can be picked until flowering, but become progressively tougher. Mint is excellent with fish, duck, tomato sauces, chilled avocado, melon and yoghurt soups, summer vegetables, rice, pasta dishes and salads. It also makes lovely sorbets, cordials, syrups, mint tea and mint vinegar. The leaves can be candied.

DILL

Dill (*Anethum graveolens*) is a delicate-looking hardy annual with sea-green, feathery leaves, similar in appearance to fennel. Its flavour is much sweeter than that of fennel, with a similar aniseed overtone. Both the leaves and seeds are used in cooking.

Cultivation: Dill does best in a sunny, well-drained soil. If you want dill leaf, choose a variety such as 'Dukat', which has larger leaves and runs to seed less quickly. If left, dill can grow well over 3 ft (1 m) tall and bolts easily in hot, dry conditions.

Sow direct from April to August in short, broad drills, 3–4 in (7.5–10 cm) wide. The seeds may take up to 14 days to germinate.

MINT RUST

This is a fungus disease which lives inside the plant, is a common problem. It appears as rust-coloured powdery spores on the underside of the leaves, and creeps up the stem, causing it to swell and twist.

● Infected plants should be dug up and burned, and new plants planted in a different position.

● The Bowles variety, *Mentha rotundifolia*, is resistant.

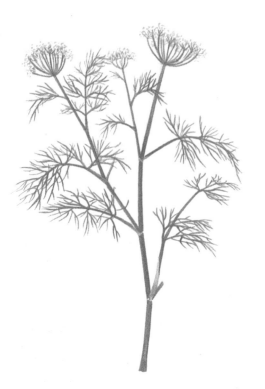

Harvesting and culinary uses: Dill is ready to cut within six to eight weeks. Pick while the leaves are young and green, taking the whole plant or cutting 1 in (2.5 cm) above the ground, when it usually resprouts. In late summer, large yellow flower heads develop. Harvest the seeds when they start to ripen and turn brown, and store somewhere cool and dry; they are sweeter in flavour than bought dill seeds. Chopped dill leaf can be added to salads, dips, yoghurt and sour cream dressings. Dill goes well with eggs, soft cheeses, fish, shellfish and cucumber; dill butter is a good accompaniment to cooked summer vegetables.

MARJORAM

Marjorams (*Origanum* species) are shrubby plants 6–24 in (15–60 cm) tall, with small woolly leaves, that bear distinc-

Keep well watered and the plants soon grow into a leafy thicket of tender leaves. No thinning is required. Alternatively, if you only want a few plants, sow a few seeds in small pots, transplanting out the young clumps with as little root disturbance as possible. If you want to grow dill for its seeds or seed heads for flower arranging, thin the plants to 9 in (23 cm) apart. Dill seeds itself readily; the seeds are long lived and are viable for at least three to five years. One to two 18 in (45 cm) rows ample.

tive 'knots' of white or pink flower clusters. Sweet or knotted marjoram is a half-hardy annual with a sweet spicy flavour, traditionally used to flavour sausages. Pot marjoram, which can be bought from a herb centre, is a hardy perennial with a stronger, coarser flavour.

Cultivation: Marjorams like full sun and poor, alkaline soils. Sow sweet marjoram in late spring under cover, thinning to 6 in (15 cm) apart. Three plants ample. Pot marjoram spreads; allow 12–24 in (30–60 cm) space for growth. One plant ample.

Harvesting and culinary uses: Pick leaves as required; they can be used (sparingly) chopped or whole for flavouring eggs, fish, lamb, tomatoes.

OREGANO

Oregano (*Origanum vulgare*) is the wild perennial form of marjoram and is the one I would most recommend. In its dried form, *rigani*, it is used for pizzas. It grows extensively in the Mediterranean, especially in Greece where its name means 'joy of the mountain'. Its small oval leaves contain thymol, a powerful antiseptic, which contributes to its strong aromatic flavour, similar to thyme but spicier. The golden variety (*Origanum vulgare aureum*) is the one I grow. It is a splendid bee plant and makes a charming rockery plant.

Cultivation: Buy a plant from the herb centre and plant out any time between spring and autumn, allowing it 12–24 in (30–60 cm) space to grow. It likes full sun and grows best in a poor, alkaline, stony soil. Once established, the plant spreads to form a compact mound. In summer, long flower stalks reaching about 9–12 in (23–30 cm) tall bear distinctive 'knots' of pink flower clusters, which bees adore. When flowering is over, cut back the old flower stalks and trim the plant to a few inches (several centimetres) above the ground. It all but dies back in winter but starts into growth in early spring. To propagate, separate a portion with its roots in spring and replant in another part of the garden.

Harvesting and culinary uses: Oregano can be picked from spring onwards and keeps its flavour well once dried. Pick regularly to encourage new young shoots to form. The stems are quite tough, so it is better to strip the leaves off by holding the stem between your finger and thumb and pulling sharply downwards. Fresh dried oregano (see p. 96) is excellent for pizzas. Oregano is also delicious with chicken and lamb, and the classic Greek salad of tomatoes, cucumber, feta cheese and black olives.

TARRAGON

Tarragon (*Artemisia dracunculus*) is one of the classic summer culinary herbs, richly aromatic, with an intriguing bitter-sweet aniseed flavour. It is a spiky plant with long needle-shaped, deep green leaves, which are rich in iodine and minerals and contain vitamins A and C. Make sure you buy French tarragon; Russian tarragon is hardier but has an inferior, coarse flavour. It can be slightly more temperamental than most herbs, but given the right conditions grows into a sizeable bush.

Cultivation: Tarragon is an almost hardy deciduous perennial. It can be grown successfully in a variety of conditions; but in cold areas it will either need winter protection, or to be grown in a container which can be brought inside during very cold weather. The plant needs a sheltered, light, well-drained soil (it will sulk in wet clay soils) and a dry, sunny position; plant out after all frosts have passed. It can reach a height of 12–24 in (30–60 cm) or more. Once established, it develops a large root ball, so allow ample room (18–24 in/45–60 cm) for growth. It deteriorates with age and should be replenished every three to four years, by taking stem cuttings or dividing the runners and replanting in a new position. The leaves become coarser and less fine-flavoured in late summer, and when the plant becomes leggy and woody; trim regularly to encourage new shoots and keep the plant bushy. Protect young shoots from slugs in spring.

Harvesting and culinary uses: Tarragon goes through three stages. The young shoots are light green, delicate and very tender. These can be picked as soon as the plant has begun to establish itself in late spring, which will encourage the stems to branch. Older leaves become darker in colour and are more aromatic but still very good. Finally, in late summer and autumn, the stems become leggy and woody and the leaves start to brown and become rank in flavour. These are not suitable for use.

Pick the sprigs just above a leaf joint to encourage further shoots. Tarragon stores well (see p. 96). It is one of the most versatile herbs and adds its own distinctive note to many dishes. Use with any meat, fish or vegetables, eggs, rice, pasta and grains. Add chopped to salads, sauces, mayonnaise and dressings.

PARSLEY

Parsley (*Petroselinum crispum*) has a fresh unobtrusive flavour that everyone likes, and is one of the most commonly used herbs everywhere. It is rich in vitamin C and stimulates digestion. It is used throughout the year, but I find it especially useful in spring or autumn. The familiar traditional curled-leaved parsley makes an excellent edging plant. I favour the curly kind, but many people find the larger continental flat-leaved parsley superior although it is slightly stronger and coarser in flavour.

Cultivation: Parsley is a hardy biennial which needs to be grown from fresh seed every year. It has long tap roots, prefers a rich, well-worked soil and can be grown in sun or shade. Sow from March to August, sowing summer batches in partially shaded spots. It is notoriously slow to germinate, especially in cold or dry conditions, and may take several weeks; soaking the seeds overnight in warm water, which softens the seed coat, is often recommended. It also needs to be nursed along in the first five to eight weeks, especially in dry or hot conditions, when it should be watered frequently.

The only way to guarantee success, I have found, is to germinate the seeds inside in

small pots. Thin to three seedlings per pot, planting out each pot when the plants are around 3 in (7.5 cm) high, allowing 9 in (23 cm) between clumps. Once established, parsley is prolific, reaching around 12 in (30 cm) tall. Because it is a biennial, it continues to grow over winter, albeit slowly. This means it is possible to have parsley all year round. For a usable winter supply, protect with cloches. Alternatively, dig up a root ball (these are larger than you imagine) and transplant into the greenhouse, or pot up and bring inside. Overwintered parsley grows rapidly in spring before finally flowering. Three clumps ample.

Harvesting and culinary uses: Wait until the plants are well established, around eight to ten weeks old, before starting to pick in earnest. Thereafter pick as required – the tender inner leaves for chopping and the older leaves for flavouring cooked dishes. The stems have a strong parsley flavour and are useful to add to stocks and soups. Parsley can be used generously in rice, pasta and grain salads and is excellent with all vegetables, fish and poultry.

BAY

The bay tree makes a handsome container-grown or tub plant to grace any patio and provide glossy, fresh aromatic leaves all year round, which are much better than packaged dried bay leaves. The flavour is similar

to mace or nutmeg with a lemony overtone. It is important to make sure you ask for, and buy, the sweet bay, *Laurus nobilis*; all other laurels are poisonous.

Cultivation: Bay is an evergreen shrub, though not entirely hardy. It can be left outside most winters but should be brought inside when temperatures drop below 5°F (−15°C). It likes full sun and a rich, well-drained soil. In the garden it can reach up to 23 ft (7 m) in height, but is usually clipped to keep it small. Both container-grown and garden-planted bay trees need trimming in spring to keep their shape.

Harvesting and culinary uses: Bay leaves can be picked and used fresh at any time of the year; they may also be dried. They are an essential ingredient of *bouquet garni*. Add to marinades, soups, stocks, stews and casseroles, stuffings, pâtés, curries, and when poaching fish, and to flavour custards, rice puddings and blancmanges.

ROSEMARY

No garden should be without rosemary (*Rosmarinus officinalis*). It is one of the most stately and aromatic of perennial herbs, long valued for its medicinal as well as culinary benefits. It can grow into a large bush, up to 6 ft (2 m) tall, and has dark green, spiky evergreen leaves which bear white, blue, pink or mauve, tiny orchid-like flowers, much loved by bees. It has a pungent flavour, strongly antiseptic but with a perfume and character all of its own. Either buy a plant from a herb centre, or get your neighbour to take a cutting for you – after all, rosemary is for remembrance. There are several varieties to choose from, including dwarf forms such as 'Suffolk Blue', and it makes a good hedge or border plant.

Cultivation: Rosemary does best in a sunny, sheltered, well-drained position and light soil. It needs lime, so add a dressing of chalk around the plant if necessary. It can be planted any time from spring to autumn. Allow 2–3 ft (60–90 cm) growing space, depending on the variety. Thereafter it needs no attention other than trimming with shears when it is large to maintain its shape.

Although generally hardy (some varieties more so than others), rosemary does not

always survive very severe weather. It is wise to take a few heel cuttings every year in May or June; or layer it any time during summer by pegging down some of the lower branches into the soil and waiting for the roots to grow. It can also become woody and may need replacing after three or four years.

Harvesting and culinary uses: Rosemary can be picked at any time of year, though young spring and summer shoots are more fragrant and the sharp spiky leaves less leathery. Strip the leaves from the stalk by pulling them hard downwards. Rosemary is excellent with fatty meats such as pork and lamb (it aids fat digestion), with chicken, veal, potatoes and squashes, and to add to wine-based meat stews or to scatter over pizzas. The flowers can be sprinkled over salads.

SAGE

Sage (*Salvia officinalis*) is a valuable blood tonic and digestive with strong antiseptic and antifungal properties, which is reflected in its unique medicinal and pungent flavour. It is also a lovely foliage and excellent bee plant, and its grey-green woolly leaves and long pinky-purple flower spikes fit well into the herbaceous border. There are many ornamental varieties of sage. For culinary purposes, I find the common broad-leaved sage and the narrow-leaved or bush sage are the best.

Cultivation: Sage prefers full sun and light, alkaline, well-drained soils. Plant any time from spring to autumn, allowing around 12 in (30 cm) for the plant to grow. It grows 12–30 in (30–75 cm) tall. Prune with shears in summer, after flowering, when the plant is large, to keep it bushy and to stimulate new growth. It is easy to propagate from heel cuttings, taken in April or May and should be replaced every three to four years when it becomes leggy and woody and shows signs of exhausting itself.

Harvesting and culinary uses: Sage is best in spring and summer when the new soft leaves form. Regular picking helps to keep the plant bushy – though often you only need two or three leaves at a time. Sage is one of the most powerful herbs and is generally used sparingly. It is excellent with pork, sausages, stuffings, veal, liver, and to flavour dried white beans. Crisp fried sage leaves are delicious.

THYME

Thyme (*Thymus*) is one of the best-known evergreen perennial culinary herbs, noted for its medicinal, digestive, preservative and antiseptic properties. Bees absolutely love it. It makes an excellent border, hedge or rockery plant, flowers profusely in summer, and is well suited to small gardens. The numerous varieties divide into two broad groups: those which have the classic thyme flavour; and other scented thymes. They are all low-growing or creeping shrubs, ranging from 3 in (7.5 cm) to 15 in (38 cm) in height, many with variegated leaves. Of the classic thymes, common garden thyme is a good all-purpose choice; of the scented kinds, one of the lemon thymes, such as 'Silver Lemon Queen', is a must. I am also very fond of the caraway thyme, a slow-growing, dwarf creeping thyme which is most attractive for small gardens.

Cultivation: Thyme succeeds best in light, well-drained, preferably alkaline soils and full sun. Cold, wet soils and dark, damp positions should be avoided. Plant out any time between spring and autumn. Depending on the ultimate size, allow 6–15 in (15–30 cm) between plants. Cut back after flowering when the plants start to get leggy, to encourage new growth. Thyme seeds itself easily in the right conditions, settling happily into any crack in paving stones. It is an evergreen perennial and may also be propagated by heel cuttings. Two to three plants sufficient.

Harvesting and culinary uses: Fresh thyme can be picked at any time of the year, but the leaves are naturally coarser and tougher during winter. It aids digestion of fats and is an invaluable herb in winter for stews, vegetable ragouts, meat broths, lamb, rabbit and game, marinades and stuffings.

6

CONTAINER VEGETABLES

Growing vegetables in containers allows you to extend the range of produce from a small garden. Crops usually reserved for the greenhouse, such as tomatoes, peppers, aubergines and cucumbers, can be raised in containers or growing bags standing on the patio or in any other sunny, sheltered spot. Potatoes and courgettes also do well in containers.

As with raised bed cultivation, you need to find out what works for you and the particular conditions in your garden. Small gardens, particularly city gardens, may have relatively large areas that are paved or concreted, and you can make productive use of that space by trying out other crops suitable for container growing. A friend recently suggested growing peas this way – and what a good idea for sugar snap peas (see p. 65). Other friends recommend small salad plants, such as rocket or land cress, or early root vegetables such as baby carrots and turnips. Climbing beans make an attractive feature in their own right, grown on cane wigwams, or up a trellis or garden wall. Many people keep herbs in pots clustered around the kitchen door, or in a window box, so that they are handy for harvesting fresh while the food is being prepared.

PREPARING THE CONTAINERS

No special skill is required, nor do you need special containers or growing mediums. Buckets, old plant pots, plastic or polystyrene packing boxes can all be used, so long as they are strong enough to carry the weight of soil or compost. The containers *must* have adequate drainage: make sure there are ample holes in the bottom and put in a layer of drainage material such as pieces of broken pots and crockery, laying the pieces carefully, convex side uppermost. Ordinary potting compost, organic compost, coir compost, or good garden soil well

Vegetables grown in coir compost thriving in containers placed in a sunny position on the patio. In the foreground are Japanese 'Slim Pim' peppers and patio tomatoes, and behind them, from left to right, yellow courgettes, aubergines and mini-cucumbers.

mixed with equal quantities of compost or peat are all suitable growing mediums. The compost must be porous, so add sufficient perlite, sand or fine gravel to soil based mixtures to lighten them; a layer of well rotted organic matter added on top of the drainage material is a good idea for deep pots. Although it's a good idea to work in a little general fertilizer such as blood, fish and bonemeal, it is false kindness to add too much, or make the container medium too rich, especially when potting young plants into large containers. They only need enough nutrients to grow. Once mature, regular supplementary feeding is best given using an appropriate liquid fertilizer.

COIR

Coir is the first major ecological alternative to peat to be produced on a large scale. It comes from waste material left after processing of the hairy fibres of coconut shells, which are used in manufacturing items such as mats and ropes. Coir looks very similar to peat and has been specially developed as an alternative base for seed and potting composts, to save continuing depletion of natural peat deposits. As a recent introduction, it initially proved hard to find, but now most garden centres stock it. I have not been using it for long, but Geoff Hamilton is an enthusiastic expert and the following is a summary of his advice. Coir can produce excellent results, but only if properly used.

● Buy a good-quality coir compost, one that carries the Coir Association logo.

● The main difference between coir and peat is that coir has a more open structure. This means that water runs through more quickly and, although coir has good moisture-retention properties, the nutrients in the compost wash out faster. To compensate for this, water pots from the bottom and incorporate a slow-release fertilizer in the potting compost. Alternatively, start feeding the plants earlier, after two to three weeks instead of six weeks.

● The top ½–1 in (1.2–2.5 cm) of coir dries out quickly, but the compost underneath is still moist. This makes it very easy to overwater. The answer is, to give less water, less often. Scratch below the surface of the compost before watering to check that the plants really do need more moisture.

MAINTENANCE OF CONTAINER VEGETABLES

The plants often need staking, and this should be done from the outset. (You will need to buy purpose-built frames for grow bags.) Tie the plants in firmly and regularly; they will be much happier if well supported than if you leave them to flop over, struggling along as best they can.

Probably the most important thing – and the only time-consuming aspect – is watering. Plants grown in containers inevitably need more watering than plants grown in the open, and lack of water causes more stress to plants than anything else. They also need more careful watering: special requirements are described in the individual plant entries that follow; for general advice on watering, see pp. 39–40.

Avoid placing containers in positions where they will be exposed to wind. Put them in the most sheltered and favourable position you can find. The other thing to remember is to keep your eyes on the plants for signs of aphids, which can sometimes be troublesome for containers kept inside, or other pests. Catch them early and they shouldn't be a problem.

RED SPIDER MITE

This is a tiny green or red mite, invisible to the naked eye, which form a fine web over the leaves of plants, causing them to become mottled and yellow. It is only a problem in hot, dry conditions. They dislike moisture: the best way to deter them is to spray the leaves regularly with water and maintain humidity levels. Persistent attacks may be biologically controlled with the parasitic mite, phytoseiulus persimilis.

TOMATOES

Tomatoes (*Lycopersicon esculentum*) originally came from South America. Like peppers, they are tender plants, need warmth and grow extremely well in containers. Modern varieties now include dwarf and compact bushy tomatoes such as 'Totem' or 'Pixie' (18–36 in/45–90 cm) for growing on patios, and a trailing variety, 'Tumbler', specifically bred for growing in hanging baskets or in flower tubs. Cherry tomatoes are superbly sweet and have twice the vitamin C content of ordinary tomatoes. 'Sweet 100' is my favourite tall variety of these, and 'Tiny Tim' (12 in/30 cm) is a good dwarf, compact variety for containers or window boxes. Of other tall varieties, I would choose yellow tomatoes, the huge beefsteak tomatoes, and those of flavour, such as 'Shirley'.

Every garden centre sells tomato plants, but rarely do they sell interesting varieties, which is a great pity. For this reason, it's better to raise tomatoes from seed. This is easy to do; stored properly, the seeds last well for two or three seasons.

Cultivation in containers: I am convinced that the best-flavoured tomatoes come from steady, unforced growth. The other secret is not to overwater the plants at any time; research now proves what many gardeners always knew – less water means better flavour.

Tomatoes need a germination temperature of around 65–70°F (18–21°C). Sow three seeds to a 3 in (7.5 cm) pot, inside from the middle to end of March, and thin to the strongest seedling. When the plants have reached 3–4 in (7.5–10 cm) high and the roots are beginning to fill the pot, after six to eight weeks, transplant into a 10 in (25 cm) pot or container; dwarf varieties like 'Totem' can go into 5–8 in (12–20 cm) pots – follow instructions on the packet. Stake the plant firmly. The tomatoes can be stood outside in a sunny, sheltered position from early June, or when the weather is suitably warm. Harden them off first (see pp. 32–3).

Dwarf and bush varieties need no further attention, except for feeding. Tall varieties should have their side-shoots pinched out as soon as they appear. This concentrates the plants' energy into producing fruit. Once they have reached around 5 ft (1.5 m) tall, pinch out the growing shoot also, which allows the remaining fruits to ripen. Tomatoes take around 16 weeks to mature and will crop steadily into early autumn. Once the first trusses have set, feed weekly with a high potash tomato fertilizer. As the season progresses, take off any dying or yellowing leaves or those showing signs of botrytis (mould) as they appear. Two to three plants minimum.

Recommended varieties: See above, plus 'Gardener's Delight' and 'Sungold' (both sweet, small fruited varieties). Yellow: 'Yellow Currant', 'Yellow Perfection', 'Mirabelle'. Beefsteak: 'Dona'.

Harvesting and culinary uses: Home-grown tomatoes are good at every stage, from barely ripe to very ripe. Barely ripe pinky tomatoes have a refreshing and thirst-quenching acidity. Perfectly ripe tomatoes have a powerful tomato scent, are richly coloured and firm, and remain so for about one week on the plant. Tomatoes left longer continue to ripen – at some stage they become mealy in texture, but make wonderful soups and fresh tomato sauce for pasta. For this reason, it's possible to leave toma-

---

PESTS AND DISEASE

The most common pest to look out for is whitefly. Potato blight (tomatoes are related to potatoes) is a fungus disease showing as brown areas on the leaf and fruit, which then rot. Spraying with a fungicide while the plants are in active growth is the best preventive measure as it can destroy the crop. Blossom end rot, fruit splitting and blossom drop are all signs of irregular watering; blossom end rot, which causes the fruit to rot, may also be due to lack of calcium.

toes on the plant and pick them as you need them. To store, don't put them in the fridge, which damages them, but keep them in a bowl in the kitchen or dining room. Home-grown tomatoes are delicious on their own or dressed with olive oil and basil. Tomato and hard-boiled egg salad is another favourite. They go especially well with chicken and fish, with other Mediterranean vegetables and any kind of cheese. Turn the surplus into soups and tomato sauce.

PEPPERS

Peppers (*Capsicum* species) are well suited to growing in containers – a certain amount of root restriction helps form the flowers and fruits. Apart from the familiar green, yellow, orange and red sweet bell peppers, which can be bought readily from garden centres, various varieties of hot peppers (*Capsicum frutescens*) are now available; if you like chilli, they are well worth trying. I also recommend the Hungarian wax pepper, which is a semi-hot sweet pepper, a compact grower (18 in/45 cm) ideal for containers; and a Japanese sweet pepper, 'Slim Pim', which is very prolific and produces slim fruits about 4 in/10 cm long. Both are available from Suffolk Herbs.

All peppers are high in vitamins C and A, and have long been valued in tropical herbal medicine for their curative properties.

Cultivation in containers: To grow well, peppers need good light, plenty of warmth and a germination temperature of 65–70°F (18–21°C); a warm airing cupboard should suffice if you have no heat. Sow two or three seeds in small pots in early to mid March. Thin to the strongest seedling, and grow on steadily. A pepper plant forms a small root ball, and doesn't like being transplanted into a large pot full of cold compost, so pot on gradually. When the plant has filled a 3 in (7.5 cm) pot, at around eight to ten weeks, transplant into a 7–10 in (18–25 cm) container. Stake firmly. Either keep growing inside or remove to the sunniest and most sheltered position sometime in June, hardening off first as necessary (see pp. 32–3).

Tie in the plants as they grow. Keep well watered and give a liquid feed with a high potash fertilizer every week once the first flower truss has set. Spraying with a fine mist helps to create the right humid atmosphere and to set the fruit. They take around 16 weeks to mature, cropping steadily thereafter, but are better brought inside once the weather turns cool. Depending on the variety, plants grow 18–24 in (45–60 cm) tall. With regular picking and feeding, each plant should bear 12 to 15 or more peppers. Two plants sufficient.

Recommended varieties: See above. Bell peppers: 'Early Prolific', 'Dwarf', 'Redskin', 'Clio', 'Triton', 'Gypsy'.

Harvesting and culinary uses: Peppers really need to be left on the plant until plump. If picked too early or too small their sweetness has not developed and the flavour can seem thin. However, to encourage more fruits to form, they must be picked regularly, so you need to strike a balance. Cut them off at the stem as you need them and store at room temperature. All peppers last and ripen well off the plant; even tiny peppers at the end of the season will ripen in due course. Raw peppers are excellent. Roasting peppers – pop them in the oven or blister the skins under the grill – softens them and brings out their sweetness; remove skins before eating. Peppers are also delicious with eggs, stuffed, or added to braised meat and poultry dishes.

AUBERGINE

Aubergine (*Solanum melongena*), or egg plant (so called because of the fruit's shape) is becoming increasingly popular with gardeners. Aubergines grow well in containers and are not difficult, but do need warmth. Unless you have a hot, sheltered spot, they really need to be grown inside in a sunny position or under glass or cloches. There are several varieties, including small-fruited types and pale, creamy-skinned varieties. The seed takes about 10 days to germinate and needs a temperature of around 60–65°F (15–18°C).

Cultivation in containers: Aubergines are grown in the same way as peppers. Sow three seeds to a 3 in (7.5 cm) pot, towards the end of March. Thin to the strongest seedling and grow on steadily – don't let the plants get leggy by giving them too much heat or too little light. Transplant into 12 in (30 cm) pots about five to six weeks later, as soon as the roots have begun to fill the pot.

Stake firmly, tying the plants in as they grow. Feed regularly with a tomato fertilizer once the flower trusses form. The general advice is to pinch out the growing tip when the plant is 10–15 in (25–38 cm) high, although it can be left to grow. Plants reach 3–4 ft (90–120 cm) tall, take about five months to mature, and will crop into early October. Allow four to six large fruits, or at least 12 to 15 of small-fruited varieties, to set; remove the rest of the flowers and pinch out side shoots as they form.

Recommended varieties: 'F1 Rima', 'Dusky', 'Slice-Rite', 'Money Maker' and 'Black Prince' (early varieties). Small-fruited varieties: 'Little Fingers', 'Short Tom', 'Easter Egg' (cream-coloured fruits).

Harvesting and culinary uses: Aubergines may be picked small or left to grow large – look for plump, firm flesh. Small-fruited varieties are best picked at about 3 in (7.5 cm) long; pick regularly to allow more fruits to form and the rest to ripen, and store at room temperature (not in the fridge) for up to two weeks. Once ready fruits should not be left on the plants too long as they may develop mould on the bottom. They are usually sliced and fried in olive oil until soft, cooked with onions, tomatoes and spices, or halved and filled with savoury rice and meat stuffings. They are also delicious cooked on the barbecue.

POTATOES

For small gardens, growing reasonable quantities of potatoes (*Solanum tuberosum*) is generally impractical. But if you want the thrill of having just a few baby new potatoes – which cost a fortune to buy – then containers provide the solution. They also produce exceptionally clean potatoes, free from pest damage.

Seed tubers are available from mid-winter to mid-spring, but are almost invariably sold in large quantities, which is uneconomic for small gardens. Ask a potato-growing neighbour to let you buy a few, share a bag of seed potatoes with friends, or ask your garden centre if they are prepared to open the bag and sell the tubers singly, which would be a big service for small gardens. If it caught on, gourmet potatoes could be sold this way – helping to preserve minority varieties and give us all more choice.

For small gardens, where the intention is just to have a few new potatoes in summer, the best idea is to plant the tubers at the traditional planting time, mid-March to April, which avoids any worry about protecting them from frosts. Ideally, use a rich compost; home-made compost is excellent. For a single tuber, a 10 in (25 cm) pot is sufficient. You can also use an old bucket, a strong fertilizer bag rolled back, or something like an old dustbin, planting 2–4 tubers depending on the size of the container. All containers should have adequate drainage holes.

Cultivation in containers: The first job is to sprout the tubers. Each tuber has most of the 'eyes' – the immature sprouts – at one end, known as the 'rose end'. Lay the tubers rose end up in a tray, such as an egg tray, in a light, cool, frost-proof place and leave until the sprouts are ½–1 in (1.2–2.5 cm) long. This takes about four to six weeks – but you can leave them much longer if convenient. Plant the tubers, sprouts facing upwards, about 4 in (10 cm) deep. Once the shoots emerge, place the containers somewhere light and sheltered, moving them outside when the weather is suitable. Protect from cold weather or late frosts if necessary by covering the containers at night or bringing inside.

Stake the plants once the foliage reaches about 9 in (23 cm) tall. It is also a good idea to 'earth up' the stems by piling more compost around them – this helps to form more potato tubers as well as giving extra support. Keep well watered, especially when the tubers are forming, around eight weeks or so after planting. It is a good idea to apply a foliar feed, or a tomato or rose feed also, to improve the weight of the crop, around this time.

Recommended varieties: Choose early potatoes. Those proven to grow well in containers include 'Epicure', 'Duke of York', 'Arran Pilot', 'Foremost' and 'Maris Bard'. A recent introduction from Marshalls (see p. 123), 'Belle de Fontenay', also works well.

Harvesting and culinary uses: For the best yields, wait until the foliage has died back, approximately 10–12 weeks after planting. The yields are variable, but each tuber should produce around 1½–2 lb (0.6–1 kg) of small potatoes, each the size of a ping-pong ball or slightly larger.

Container grown potatoes need only a quick wash. Steam them or wrap in foil and bake in the oven with a sprig of mint.

If you want, save a few of the harvested tubers and pot them up in August as before, bringing them inside to a light position when the weather turns cool, to give you new potatoes for Christmas.

Cucurbits

Cucurbits include courgettes, cucumbers, gherkins, marrows, summer and winter squashes, and pumpkins. They are all large trailing or bushy plants, prolific and decorative. Most have hairy prickly leaves and tendrils and come from warmer climates. They can be grown up a trellis or in containers. I have provided instructions here for growing cucumbers and courgettes in containers or in a bed.

All cucurbits need germination temperatures around 65–70°F (18–21°C), rich soil, a sunny position and copious watering once the fruit begins to set. They dislike any root disturbance, will sulk in cold, wet or heavy soils and in windy positions. Because they have a long cropping season and need warmth, generally it is better to start them off inside. They are also prone to mildew and dampening off in the early stages of growth – this can largely be prevented by taking care not to overwater and by keeping the plants well ventilated.

COURGETTES

Courgettes (*Cucurbita pepo*) are very popular – and grow into very large plants. For small gardens, grow them in the herbaceous border, or any suitable odd corner and choose some of the more unusual kinds, which you cannot buy. The 'F1 Supremo' mini-courgette is a compact variety specially bred for small gardens, and is very suitable for growing in containers.

Cultivation in containers: Whether you grow them in containers or in the garden, it is a mistake to start courgettes or any kind of squash too early. For containers, sow two to three seeds inside, ½ in (1.2 cm) deep on their edge in 3 in (7.5 cm) pots, in mid to late April. Discard any stunted-looking seedlings, thin to the strongest one and grow steadily; do not overwater at this stage. When the roots have begun to fill the pot, transplant into a 10–12 in (25–30 cm) container. Alternatively, you can sow three seeds direct into a large container, thinning to the strongest seedling. Harden off and place in a sunny sheltered position from the

end of May to early June, protected if necessary with a piece of horticultural fleece. Keep well watered, and give a liquid feed as necessary.

Cultivation outside: Sow individual seeds as above and grow on steadily as before. Plant out four to five weeks later, but only when the soil is warm the weather is suitable, hardening them off first (see pp. 32–3) – be guided by the season and your growing conditions: if you sow too early, you may have to delay planting out time, and the plants may become pot-bound. Make sure the stem is proud of the soil, otherwise stem

rot may set in. Protect with a cloche until the plant is growing well.

In mild districts, seeds can be sown outdoors from the middle to end of May under a mini-cloche, such as a large jam jar or cut-off plastic bottle put in place a week before sowing to warm up the soil. Remove the mini-cloches once the plants have two true leaves, or the young plant begins to touch the sides, replacing with a larger cloche. Protect all young plants from slugs. Courgettes are slow-growing at first, but quicken once the temperatures start to rise. Keep well watered (see pp. 39–40). If you can, keep them mulched once the weather gets hot. They take around 12 weeks to mature and can easily reach 2 ft (60 cm) tall and wide – hack back some of the leaves if the plant gets out of hand. If picked regularly they should continue cropping until early autumn. One or two plants sufficient.

Recommended varieties: 'F1 Clarella', 'Gold Rush', 'F1 Supremo'; Summer squashes: 'Custard White', 'F1 Sunburst'.

Harvesting and culinary uses: Courgettes are best young and tender, at any size from the thickness of your middle finger, and 3–4 in (7.5–10 cm) long to around 6 in (15 cm). Like this, they have a creamy flesh and mild, delicate taste. Smaller than this, I find them lacking in flavour. Larger ones, by contrast, can be watery and slightly bitter in flavour.

Courgettes must be picked regularly – turn your back and you have a marrow on your hands. Cut them at the stem and bring inside. Store somewhere cool, not in the fridge which makes them rubbery and dulls the flavour. Use raw in salads, sliced thinly. They can be stuffed with rice or meat mixtures and braised with other vegetables such as tomatoes and peppers; the scalloped-edged summer squashes are particularly attractive cooked like this. Courgette flowers are edible (and delicious) and may be deep-fried or stuffed. Pick them when they have just opened, and check for any insects. Bring inside and wrap gently in cling film immediately.

CUCUMBER

Generally speaking, home-grown cucumbers (*Cucumis sativus*) have a much better flavour and are much juicier than bought cucumbers. Smooth 'greengrocer' cucumbers need a greenhouse and specialist treatment. 'Outdoor' or 'ridge' cucumbers have thicker, prickly skins, are excellent to eat, and grow successfully outdoors in mild areas, though they do not do well in cold summers. I would not recommend them for northern or cold districts. My favourites are the Japanese type of outdoor cucumber such as 'Kyoto', or the 'F1 Burpless' varieties such as 'Burpless Tasty Green'. These are trailing cucumbers 4–6 ft (1.2–2 m) tall and must be grown up a frame of some kind (keep well tied in), but they have an excellent flavour and are never bitter. They produce long cucumbers and crop well even in cold summers. Trailing cucumbers also include gherkin cucumbers, the unusual round-fruited crystal apple cucumber and mini-cucumbers, small-fruited cucumbers which reach about 5 ft (1.5 m) tall. For small gardens, compact outdoor bush cucumbers are also a good choice. All cucumbers grow well in containers. Germination takes about nine days and needs a temperature around 70°F (21°C).

Cultivation in containers: Sow two or three seeds inside, ½ in (1.2 cm) deep on their edge in 3 in (7.5 cm) pots, from mid-April to early May. Thin to the strongest seedling. Keep the compost barely moist in the early stages of growth. When the plants have formed a good root system and have three or four true leaves (around four to five weeks), transplant each very carefully into a 10 in (25 cm) container and stake. Put outside in a sunny sheltered position from early June, hardening off first (see p. 32).

Cucumbers are greedy feeders and very thirsty. Once the fruits have started to form, give a liquid feed every seven to ten days with a high potash fertilizer and water copiously, preferably with slightly warmed water. They take around 12 weeks to mature, and should crop steadily into September. Bush varieties grow to around 18 in (45 cm) in height and spread. One plant sufficient.

Cultivation outside: Bush and ridge cucumbers for growing outside need a rich, friable, moisture-holding soil – prepare individual holes 12 in (30 cm) deep and 18 in (45 cm) wide and fill with organic or garden compost. Sow the seeds as above – as for courgettes, not too early – and grow on steadily in their 3 in (7.5 cm) pots. Plant out carefully in the prepared planting holes in early June when the weather is mild, when the plant is 3–4 in (7.5–10 cm) high, or when the roots are beginning to fill the pot. Allow space for growth 18 in (45 cm) for trailing or climbing types and 2 ft (60 cm) for bush types. Cover with cloches until the plant is well established and protect from slugs. If growing trailing varieties up canes, tie firmly every 6–8 in (15–20 cm) so that fruits are well supported.

Recommended varieties: (for containers and growing outside) Outdoor bush cucumber: 'Bush Champion'. Japanese outdoor cucumber: 'Burpless Tasty Green', 'Kyoto', 'Gherkin', 'Hokus', 'Venlo Pickling'. Mini-cucumber: 'Petita F1', 'Sweet Alphee F1'. Note that F1 hybrids have as few as five seeds per packet.

Harvesting and culinary uses: Ideally, cucumbers should be picked just before they are eaten. They must also be picked regularly to encourage more fruits to form. Cut them at about 9–12 in (23–30 cm) long and when they are nicely plump; don't let them get too big, as the seeds become too large. Mini-cucumbers ought to be cut at no more than 6 in (15 cm) long, though I find them better if left to grow slightly larger, up to 9 in (23 cm). Cucumbers store very well for a few days in a cool place; don't put them in the fridge, which is damaging. Peel the skins if very tough. Diced cucumber makes a marvellous, refreshing addition to summer salads and salads based on rice. It also makes excellent soups or stir-fried and served with fish or chicken.

DISEASES

Apart from mildew and dampening off (see above), check for aphids which collect on the underside of the leaves. Cucumber mosaic virus disease causes mottled and yellowed leaves and stunted plants; destroy the plants. Some varieties e.g. 'Bush Champion' and mini-cucumbers are disease resistant.

USEFUL BOOKS

Know and Grow Vegetables, Part 1 and *Part 2*, P. J. Salter, J. K. A. Bleasdale, and others, National Vegetable Research Station, Oxford University Press.

Beds, Pauline Pears, Henry Doubleday Research Association/Search Press.

Step-by-Step Organic Gardening Series, illustrated booklets (8–16 pages), Henry Doubleday Research Association. Single copies available from: The Organic Gardening Catalogue, Chase Organics (GB) Ltd, Addlestone, Surrey KT15 1HY. In particular:
Growing From Seed;
Composting;
Making Worm Compost;
Pest Control Without Poisons;
On the Slug Trail;
Weed Control Without Chemicals.

Successful Organic Gardening, Geoff Hamilton, Dorling Kindersley.

The Salad Garden, Joy Larkcom, Windward Press.

The Complete Book of Herbs, Lesley Bremness, Dorling Kindersley in association with the National Trust.

USEFUL ADRESSES

ORGANIZATIONS

The Henry Doubleday Research
Association
Ryton Gardens
Ryton-on-Dunsmore
Coventry CV8 3LG

Wessex Environmental Consultancy
Bath College of Higher Education
Newton Park
Bath BA2 9BN
(Soil and lead analysis).

SUPPLIERS

A. R. Paske
Regal Lodge
Kentford
Newmarket
Suffolk CB8 7QB
(Seakale)

Hollington Nurseries
Woolton Hill
Newbury
Berkshire RG15 9XT
(Herbs)

SEEDSMEN

Samuel Dobie & Son Ltd
Broomhill Way
Torquay
Devon TQ2 7QW

Suffolk Herbs
Monks Farm
Pantlings Lane
Kelvedon
Essex CO5 9PG
(Unusual salad plants and
vegetables)

Unwins Seeds Ltd
Histon
Cambridge CB4 4ZZ

Chase Organics (GB) Ltd
Coombelands House
Coombelands Lane
Addlestone
Weybridge KT15 1HY
(Organic gardening
catalogue and seeds)

S. E. Marshall & Co Ltd
Wisbech
Cambs PE13 2RF

Suttons Seeds Ltd
Hele Road
Torquay
Devon TQ2 7QJ

Thompson & Morgan
London Road
Ipswich IP2 0BA

Kings Crown of Kelvedon
E. W. King & Co. Ltd
Coggeshall Road
Kelvedon
Essex CO5 9PG

INDEX

Page numbers in *italic* refer to illustrations

GARDENERS' WORLD BOOK OF
BULBS

by SUE PHILLIPS

GARDENERS' WORLD BOOK OF
CONTAINER GARDENING

by ANNE SWITHINBANK

GARDENERS' WORLD BOOK OF
HOUSEPLANTS

by ANNE SWITHINBANK

GARDENERS' WORLD
PLANTS FOR SMALL GARDENS

by SUE FISHER